Volume 1

Child Abuse

CURRENT ISSUES

CURRENT ISSUES

CURRENT ISSUES

CURRENT ISSUES

CURRENT ISSUES

CURRENT ISSUES

Volume 1

Child Abuse

WITHDRAWN

By
Richard Layman

Omnigraphics, Inc.

Penobscot Building • Detroit, MI 48226

For
Mary A. Layman
Who has proven her strength again
in a very difficult year

ISBN 1-55888-271-5

Table of Contents

this interview, she describes her approach to therapy, how she prepares children to testify against abusers, her experience with child protective services, and the child's perspective on maltreatment.

- History
- Response to a Report
- Substantiation
- Caseworkers' Dilemma
- The Rights of Children
- The Rights of Parents
- The Rights of Guardians

- With extensive experience in the field of criminal abuse and neglect, Andrew Vachss is an outspoken critic of inadequate response to the maltreatment of children. He discusses how the legal system deals with child victims, the nature of the advocacy provided to them, the motivation of pedophiles and child pornographers, and the kind of public response required to bring about reforms.

- Criminal Court
- Civil Actions
- Divorce Court
- Family Court
- Parental Custody
- Revocation of Custody
- Imminent Danger
- Other Reasons for Revoking Custody
- General Works Useful to the Nonspecialist, on the Subject of Child Maltreatment, With Order Information

- James M. Peters is senior attorney with the National Center for Prosecution of Child Abuse, a branch of the National District Attorney's Association. He is an experienced criminal prosecutor who presently devotes much of his time to providing technical assistance, advice about trial strategy, and training to local prosecutors. Mr. Peters helped draft the Child Victim's "Bill of Rights" which is being considered by Congress in 1990.

Acknowledgments

This book was produced by Manly, Inc., and designed by Quentin Fiore. Jean W. Ross was the project director; she gathered research materials, contacted advisors, and assisted materially in every step of production. George F. Dodge was the typographer; his mastery of the microcomputer made it possible to produce this book quickly and efficiently. Jim Hipp was the production supervisor; he ensured that details were not overlooked. Bill Adams was the proofing supervisor; his able department includes Rowena Betts, Anne L. M. Bowman, Patricia Coate, David Marshall James, Laura Garren Moore, and Betsy L. Weinberg. Essential library research was provided by Walter W. Ross and Parris Boyd.

The author owes an unusually large debt to the many advisors—both librarians and workers in the field of child abuse and neglect—who responded patiently, intelligently, and fully to the many queries presented to them. Special thanks are due the following people who provided expert counsel, in addition to that of the vettors: Lois W. Abramczyk, MSSW, Ed.D., Director of The Center for Child and Family Studies, University of South Carolina; Wilbert Lewis, Director, Child Protective and Preventive Services, South Carolina Department of Social Services; Jane D. Griffin, Director, Lexington County, S.C., Public Library; and Marianne White, Western Area Librarian, Henrico County, Virginia, Public Library System.

Series Description

Current Issues has a simply stated purpose: to provide in an orderly way the information necessary to discuss and pursue matters of public concern intelligently. Topics are chosen for their significance, their interest, and their relevance to contemporary life—in the United States and throughout the world.

Purpose

Each volume of *Current Issues* will provide balanced information about a single topic in an unbiased manner. The first element of each book is the Statement of the Issue, in which the topic is introduced and the boundaries of its discussion are stipulated. Definition of key terms related to the issue is always an important element in *CI* entries.

Definition

After definition comes description. What information—statistics, studies, and reports, for example—is available to describe how the issue under discussion affects contemporary life? The limits of this information and its usefulness are indicated where possible. A key element of each book is original, in-depth interviews with spokesmen associated with the topic. Interview subjects are chosen to represent different viewpoints and to elucidate different aspects of the issue under discussion. These interviews are not intended to be argumentative, but rather to present a specialist's perspective.

Entry Content: Description; Interview

A checklist of resource materials, a directory of organizations, and a bibliography are provided to guide the user interested in gathering information related to the topic. The list of resource materials is not limited to what might be found in a public or university library. Useful fact sheets and information packets provided by organizations, both private and public, are cited, and order information is included. The guide to organizations provides addresses, phone numbers, contact persons (when available), and a description of the nature and activities of key groups active in the field under discussion. The bibliography is a selective guide to useful books on the subject.

Entry Content: Checklist; Directory

Each volume of *Current Issues* is sent to experts for their comments about the balance and accuracy of the material presented and their suggestions for revision. In most cases, these suggestions are taken into account in the final editing of the book. In certain cases, however, it is not feasible for some reason to heed the advice of a vettor. In such a case, the vettor is given an opportunity to comment critically on the material presented.

Entry Content: Vetting

The goal of *Current Issues* volumes is to present accurate information objectively. When there is an honest difference of opinion among knowledgeable commentators, the reader has a right to know.

Entry Format and Index

A successful reference book has two obligations: to provide reliable information and to present it in a usable format. Careful consideration has been given to the format of *CI* in order to make the body of information provided as usable and as useful as possible. The format was designed with two types of users in mind: the user who will read an entry or group of entries thoroughly to assimilate all of the information provided; and the quick-reference user who will return to an entry to find a piece of information quickly or who will scan an entry for information of interest. Liberal use is made of rubrics and headings in *CI*. Information is useless if it is not accessible, and thus indexing is central to the rationale of *CI*. Full proper name and subject indexes are provided for each volume. Indexes on related topics will be cumulated and cross-referenced.

Audience

It is expected that *Current Issues* will prove useful to a varied audience: high school and college students doing reports and research assignments, library patrons in search of reliable information on issues in the news, teachers seeking a resource for classroom presentations, group leaders requiring material for civic discusssion groups. The test of this series is its utility. The publisher and the editors are confident of meeting that test.

1

Statement of Issue

There is general agreement in America that child abuse is a compelling problem that requires focused attention and decisive action. There is not general agreement about what precisely child abuse is. Even among professionals working with maltreated children, the term has different meanings.

The Child Abuse and Treatment Act of 1974, the federal law which stimulated the gargantuan development of state child protective services (CPS)* agencies, stipulates that for its purposes, child abuse (and its complement neglect) "means the physical or mental injury, sexual abuse, negligent treatment, or maltreatment of a child under the age of eighteen by a person who is responsible for the child's welfare under circumstances which indicate that the child's health or welfare is harmed or threatened thereby, as determined in accordance with regulations prescribed by the Secretary [of Health, Education, and Welfare]." By this definition, a young boy molested by a stranger is not a victim of child abuse, because the molester is not responsible for the boy's welfare.

But the molester is a criminal. A crime against a child is normally a crime regardless of the criminal's relationship to the victim, and, if the crime involves physical maltreatment, it is called child abuse in court. The molester in the example above is, to be sure, subject to criminal indictment, just as a parent or guardian would be who violated a criminal law by abusing his or her child—by killing or maiming or raping the child, for example. In most states the law stipulates that such criminals will be registered in a statewide database, which may also include people accused of noncriminal maltreatment. In some states the child abuse registry must be consulted by employers

---

* Child protective services is the name given to the specialized state and community-level units that usually operate as divisions of departments of social services or law enforcement agencies to provide for the welfare of children, particularly with regard to abuse and neglect within the family.

before they hire anyone engaged in work related to children.

**Activist's
Usage**

Public interest groups, who are not charged with the duty of enforcing specific laws, often adopt their own definitions that interpret child maltreatment as a general description of behavior. There are many different private organizations devoted to addressing the issue of child maltreatment, and they represent a broad range of philosophies about the role of children and parents in contemporary society. The National Committee for Prevention of Child Abuse, for example, defines child abuse in broad terms as "a nonaccidental injury or pattern of injuries to a child." VOCAL (Victims of Child Abuse Laws), on the other hand, argues for a very restrictive definition assuming that false allegations will be reduced as a result.

**Who Is
a Child?**

There is also the matter of who is considered to be a child. The Child Abuse and Treatment Act defines a child as anyone "under the age of eighteen." Criminal laws vary from state to state, but in most states no distinction is drawn between child and adult victims. Children are protected by the same laws that protect adults. (There are, of course, exceptions—notably statutory rape, which outlaws sexual relations between an adult and a child under a certain age that varies with state law.) Public interest groups tend to be imprecise in defining who is a child, considering circumstances of the maltreatment in their determination: moderate corporal punishment, while frowned upon, might be considered abusive for a six-month-old but not for a twelve-year-old, for example. (No state law expressly prohibits corporal punishment, and in Colorado, Ohio, Oklahoma, South Carolina, and Washington, the law explicitly states that reasonable corporal punishment by parents or guardians is permitted. In 26 other states, the law permits reasonable force on the part of a caretaker to maintain discipline.)

**Background
of Abuse
and Neglect
Laws**

Until the mid 1960s there were relatively few laws that specifically addressed the maltreatment of children. It was, of course, illegal to murder, assault, or rape a child, and a body of child labor laws had been enacted in response to the abuses of the industrial revolution, but, generally, the less debilitating forms of physical abuse, most forms of emotional maltreatment, and nearly all forms of neglect, as it is presently construed, were considered outside the realm of the law. The purpose of the laws that did exist was typically to provide for punishment of the wrongdoer rather than protection for the victim.

illegal to murder, assault, or rape a child, and a body of child labor laws had been enacted in response to the abuses of the industrial revolution, but, generally, the less debilitating forms of physical abuse, most forms of emotional maltreatment, and nearly all forms of neglect, as it is presently construed, were considered outside the realm of the law. The purpose of the laws that did exist was typically to provide for punishment of the wrongdoer rather than protection for the victim.

Moreover, the roles of children within the family unit were considered to be a matter left almost entirely to parents (or substitute caretakers), even if the children appeared to suffer as a result. Yet, while parents were acknowledged to be largely responsible for their children's behavior, there was little legislation that specifically vested parents, guardians, or other caretakers with responsibilities for a child's welfare and made failure to discharge those responsiblilites unlawful.

General Abuse and Neglect Laws

In the early 1960s states and the federal government began to accept the notion that children have rights within the family that require legal protection. The culmination of this attitude was the 1974 Child Abuse and Treatment Act, (amended in 1978, 1984, and 1988), which formally defined child abuse and neglect, provided federal funds to address the issue, and encouraged states to pass comprehensive laws against child maltreatment by withholding money if they failed to enact appropriate legislation. Using federal laws as a basis, separate statutes in every state now define child maltreatment in language that is generally uniform: It is safe to say that in the United States, unlawful child maltreatment is the abuse or neglect of a child under the age of eighteen by a parent, guardian, or some other person responsible for the child's welfare. It is a violation of trust, and it is the infliction of harm. Maltreatment laws cover commisive acts (abuse) and omissive acts (neglect). Yet while maltreatment is illegal, it is not normally addressed in criminal court. Child abuse and neglect laws exist to protect the child and to help, rather than punish, the abuser.

Most of the information included here relates to abuse and neglect in the United States as defined by the 1974 Child Abuse and Treatment Act and its amendments. The best and most reliable sources for information about child maltreatment are the reports to state departments of social services, incomplete as they are and misleading as they can be. The focus of this discussion, then, is on reported child maltreatment committed by a parent or some other caretaker. It must always be kept in mind, however, that some professionals who do not work di-

Discussion Boundaries

rectly with CPS accept a different definition. Because of the difficulty of gathering reliable statistics, numbers are often deceptive in describing the incidence of child abuse and neglect; however, respected studies conducted by the American Association for Protecting Children (a division of the American Humane Association) show that in 1987 just under 2.2 million cases of child maltreatment were reported to state agencies in the United States, and some 1,200 children were recognized by authorities as having died because of abusive treatment by adults. Reports were filed on 1.4 million families, and, though only some 40% of these reports resulted in full investigation that verified the occurrence of abuse or neglect, authorities believe that only a small fraction of all occurrences are reported, a maximum of one-third by conservative estimate. Public awareness of the problem is suggested by the fact that there was a 226% increase in the number of cases of child abuse and neglect reported to CPS between 1976 and 1987.

Shift in Perspective

Alfred Kadushin points out in *Child Welfare Services* (NY: Macmillan, 1980) that the recent interest in child maltreatment may be traced to the focused attention of the medical profession on the battered child during the 1960s and 1970s. Particularly influential were Dr. C. Henry Kempe and his associates at the University of Colorado School of Medicine, who studied the recurrence of child battery and energetically publicized their findings. (See Chapter 4.) Thus the orientation of the social worker, which had affected public opinion about child maltreatment to that time, was replaced by a perception of the issue in more specific medical terms, prompting congressional hearings and subsequent legislation aimed at encouraging aggressive action by states. House and Senate investigations led to passage of the 1974 Child Abuse Prevention and Treatment Act (Public Law 93-247), which essentially had three effects.

1974 Federal Law

1) It established the National Center on Child Abuse and Neglect, an agency under the auspices of the Secretary of Health, Education, and Welfare, to compile, analyze, and publish research; develop and maintain an information clearinghouse on both private and public programs; compile and publish training materials for child protective services personnel; provide technical assistance to agencies addressing the issue of child maltreatment; conduct original research; and conduct a national incidence study.

2) It enacted guidelines which states had to meet in order to receive federal funding. States had to: mandate the reporting of suspected or verified cases of maltreatment; provide immunity from prosecution for persons reporting maltreatment; provide a means (such as a hotline) for such reporting; provide for investigation of reports; demonstrate the existence of administrative procedures and personnel to deal effectively with maltreatment cases; assure confidentiality of records; provide for cooperation among human services agencies and courts; provide for guardians ad litem*; provide for the education of the general public; and encourage the development of programs by parental organizations.

3) It provided funding: $15 million in 1973-1974; increasing to $25 million in 1975-1976.

Federal Amendments

The Child Abuse Prevention and Treatment and Adoption Reform Acts of 1978, 1984, and 1988 amend the 1974 law in ways that may be described as fine-tuning. Funding is extended, studies are required, and, in the 1978 Act, legislation is added to simplify the procedure for adoption of children in foster homes. Administrative details, such as the methods for approving grants and study topics, including how to improve the ad litem program, are directed by the 1988 act, which also establishes a National Commission on Child and Youth Deaths, a Presidential advisory panel. The 1988 funding level was $48 million.

Differing Views

Child maltreatment is an emotionally charged issue. As an irresponsible exercise of power—the victimization of children by the adults who have the moral and legal obligation to protect them—child abuse invites an indignant response. Yet, while some activists claim that too few resources are brought to bear on a matter that directly affects the future of our society, others argue that the issue elicits irrational responses, inviting overly zealous action that may deprive accused abusers of their rights, promote the passage of unduly restrictive laws, and violate the privacy of families.

---

*A guardian ad litem is a court-appointed advocate for a child in court proceedings in which the child is involved. The guardian ad litem may or may not be an attorney, depending on the state; most often the job is performed by a lay volunteer. The duties and responsibilities of guardians ad litem vary greatly throughout the United States, as do qualifications for people who wish to serve in that capacity.

2

Definitions of Key Terms

Introduction   The discussion of child abuse and neglect is clouded by the difficulty of defining key terms and describing basic concepts underlying the problem. The types of behavior that are considered to be abusive or neglectful differ from culture to culture and evolve historically; attitudes about the rights of children vary among social classes, religious denominations, and ethnic groups.

Legal Definitions   The National Center on Child Abuse and Neglect, a division of the U.S. Department of Health and Human Services, points out that "each state has its own definitions which, while incorporating the Federal definition, may vary in other ways from State to State. Even beyond the official definitions established by Federal and State laws, Child protective services agencies, professionals in schools, hospitals, mental health agencies and child care centers appear to have widely differing interpretations of these laws regarding the types and severity of child maltreatment, what needs to be reported, and how to treat it."

A state-by-state compendium of laws is provided in *State Statutes Related to Child Abuse and Neglect 1988*. This 1989 publication (#06-88098) of the U.S. Department of Health and Human Services is available for $80 from the Clearinghouse on Child Abuse and Neglect Information, PO Box 1182, Washington, DC 20013.

Categories of Abuse and Neglect   The federal law recognizes three categories of child abuse and three of neglect, described in the National Center on Child Abuse and Neglect *Study Findings: Study of National Incidence and Prevalence of Child Abuse and Neglect: 1988* (see pp. 20-21), which also estimates the annual occurrences of each category of abuse. The definitions and estimates below are quoted or paraphrased from that report. It should be noted that the estimates are of cases known to state child protective agencies, investigatory agencies, or professionals in community institutions, such as schools or hospitals.

1) Physical abuse is the mistreatment of a child that causes physical injury, impairment, or endangerment.
1,584,700 cases were estimated in 1986.

Physical Abuse

2) Sexual abuse is divided into three subcategories:

Sexual Abuse

a) Intrusion, which means evidence of actual penile penetration, whether oral, anal, or genital, homosexual or heterosexual.
48,400 cases were estimated in 1986.

b) Molestation with genital contact, which means some form of genital contact without specific indication of intrusion.
70,300 cases were estimated in 1986.

c) Other sexual abuse, which means acts such as fondling not known to have involved genital contact or inadequate or inappropriate supervision of a child's voluntary sexual activities.
37,600 cases were estimated in 1986.

3) Emotional abuse is divided into three subcategories:

Emotional Abuse

a) Close confinement, which is a torturous restriction of movement, such as tying or binding a child or confining a child to an enclosed area as a means of punishment.
11,100 cases were estimated in 1986.

b) Verbal or emotional assault, which is habitual patterns of belittling, denigrating, or other forms of overtly hostile or rejecting treatment.
144,300 cases were estimated in 1986 .

c) Other abuse, which is other overtly punitive, exploitative, or abusive treatment, for example, attempted or potential assault; deliberate withholding of food, sleep, shelter, or other necessities as a form of punishment; and economic exploitation.
63,200 cases were estimated in 1986.

4) Physical neglect is divided into seven subcategories:

Physical Neglect

a) Refusal of health care, which is failure to provide or allow care for an injury, illness, or medical condition in accordance with the recommendations of health care professionals.
71,600 cases were estimated in 1986.

b) Delay in health care, which is the failure to seek

appropriate medical care for a serious health problem that any reasonable person would recognize as needing professional attention.
37,300 cases were estimated in 1986.

c) Abandonment/desertion of a child, including cases in which children are left for at least two days by persons responsible for a child's welfare who do not leave information about their own whereabouts.
17,100 cases were estimated in 1986.

d) Expulsion, which means the blatant refusal to provide care for a child or to make adequate arrangements for care by others. Expulsion includes the refusal to accept custody of a returned runaway.
45,300 cases were estimated in 1986.

e) Other custody-related issues, which are custody-related forms of inattention to a child's needs other than abandonment or expulsion—chronically and repeatedly leaving a child with others, for example.
34,300 cases were estimated in 1986.

f) Inadequate supervision, which is leaving a child unsupervised or inadequately supervised for extended periods or allowing a child to remain away from home for extended periods without knowing his whereabouts.
192,100 cases were estimated in 1986.

g) Other physical neglect, which is conspicuous inattention to avoidable hazards; inadequate nutrition, clothing, or hygiene; or reckless endangerment, such as driving while drunk with a child in the car, or leaving a young child unattended in a car.
223,500 cases were estimated in 1986.

Educational Neglect

5) Educational neglect is divided into three subcategories:

a) Permitted chronic truancy, which is habitual truancy of at least five days per month that the parent or guardian does not attempt to rectify after having been informed.
220,000 cases were estimated in 1986.

b) Failure to enroll/other truancy, which is the failure to enroll a child of mandatory school age and causing him to miss at least one month of school; or keeping a school-age child out of school for nonlegitimate reasons, such as to work or care for a sibling, on an average of at least

three days a month.
66,600 cases were estimated in 1986.

c) Inattention to a special educational need, which is the failure to obtain recommended remedial educational services or treatment for a diagnosed learning disability without reasonable cause.
6,000 cases were estimated in 1986.

6) Emotional neglect is divided into seven subcategories:

Emotional Neglect

a) Inadequate nurturance/affection, which is a marked inattention to the child's need for affection, emotional support, attention, or competence.
48,500 cases were estimated in 1986.

b) Chronic /extreme spouse abuse, which is domestic violence in the presence of a child.
27,100 cases were estimated in 1986.

c) Permitted drug/alcohol abuse, which means permitting drug or alcohol abuse by a child.
44,900 cases were estimated in 1986.

d) Permitted other maladaptive behavior, which is encouraging or permitting delinquency.
24,200 cases were estimated in 1986.

e) Refusal of psychological care, which is refusing to allow needed treatment for a child's emotional or behavioral impairment in accordance with professional counsel.
24,400 cases were estimated in 1986.

f) Delay in psychological care, which is the failure to seek or provide such care, as in the case of clinical depression or attempted suicide.
25,700 cases were estimated in 1986.

g) Other emotional neglect, which is inattention to the child's developmental or emotional needs not covered by other subcategories, such as fostering immaturity or overdependence; or applying expectations clearly inappropriate to the child's age or level of development.
57,600 cases were estimated in 1986.

7) Other maltreatment is divided into two subcategories:

Other Maltreatment

a) General or unspecified neglect, which covers neglect allegations not classifiable elsewhere, such as failure to provide preventive health care or multiple neglect

allegations not included under any single category above.
38,600 cases were estimated in 1986.

b) Other or unspecified maltreatment, which covers
allegations not classifiable elsewhere, such as parent or
guardian behavior that affects the child, including
prostitution or drug abuse.
44,300 cases were estimated in 1986.

3

Statistics

While there is general agreement that child maltreatment is a national problem of large proportions, it is difficult to describe its magnitude because of inadequate information. The two most ambitious and reliable surveys are funded by the U.S. Department of Health and Human Services. One of these surveys, conducted by the American Humane Association, deals only with cases actually reported to child protective agencies. Its advantage is that it analyzes real data, eliminating the guesswork of estimation. Its disadvantage is that by considering only reported cases, it ignores an estimated two-thirds of all occurrences of maltreatment.

The other of these surveys, conducted by the National Center on Child Abuse and Neglect, includes all cases of child abuse and neglect known to professionals who have contact with children. Its advantage is that it considers occurrences, not just reports. Its disadvantage is that it is based on a statistical sampling of twenty-nine representative counties in the United States, and it is limited by the reliability of the statistical sample.

With funding from the National Center on Child Abuse and Neglect of the Department of Health and Human Services, the American Humane Association has since 1974 gathered and analyzed official reports of child maltreatment submitted by state departments of social services. The most recent survey indicates that 2,178,000 reports of child abuse and neglect were filed nationwide in 1987—that is, 34 reports per 1000 children in the general population. The American Humane Association states that, based on survey data from the thirty states in which it was available, 40 to 42% of the cases reported were substantiated* by CPS in 1986.

Magnitude

American Humane Association Survey

---

*The terms "founded" and "substantiated" are used to describe those cases in which child protective agency workers determine after investigation that abuse has occurred. That determination is subject to judicial review and may be reversed.

That statistic indicates that by conservative estimate 737,000 children were judged by CPS to be victims of child abuse or neglect.

A Statistical Profile of Child Maltreatment Victims and Their Families—1986 (American Humane Association Findings)

■ The average age of the child was 7.2 years (43% under five; 33% between six and eleven; 24% between twelve and seventeen).

■ 52.5% of the victims were girls.

■ 65.5% of the victims were white; 20.5% were black; 10.8% were Hispanic.

■ There were an average of 2.21 children in the maltreated child's household.

■ 48.9% of the families were on public assistance.

■ 32.5% of the families were headed by a single female.

■ The average age of the abuser was 31.7.

■ 55.9% of the abusers were women.

This report, *Highlights of Official Child Abuse Reporting, 1986*, is available for $16, plus postage from the American Humane Association, 9720 East Hampton Ave., Denver, CO 80231-4919

*   *   *

National Center on Child Abuse

Under the requirements of the Child Abuse Prevention and Treatment Act, the National Center on Child Abuse and Neglect has compiled two national surveys on child maltreatment, one in 1979-1980 and one in 1988. Unlike the American

---

To say that a case is unfounded does not mean that the report of maltreatment was determined to have been false. Action in the case may have been suspended because the victim or the accused left the jurisdiction of the reporting agency, or for many other reasons.

Humane Association survey, these reports are estimates drawn from studies in twenty-nine statistically representative counties in the United States. Called National Incidence Studies, these surveys attempt to go beyond formally filed reports to include cases of child abuse known to have occurred and yet not reported to CPS. They also are able to eliminate reports without merit. Whereas about 40% of the reports in the American Humane Association study are "substantiated," 73% in the National Incidence Study are believed to be verifiable, and 15% are of undetermined status. Interestingly, this study indicated that many professionals failed to report suspected abuse or neglect to CPS or to law enforcement agencies—in violation of federal law, which mandates reporting.

> The 1988 *Study of National Incidence and Prevalence of Child Abuse and Neglect* reported the following conclusions:

National Incidence Study–1988 Conclusions

■ Over one million children nationwide have suffered demonstrable harm as a result of abusive treatment.

■ The incidence of abuse and neglect is about equal, and in both categories, children are more likely to be victims of physical mistreatment than other forms.

■ Public school teachers and administrators report about half of all the cases of abuse and neglect known to child protective agencies; school personnel also fail to report about half of the cases known to them.

■ The dramatic increase in the known incidence of child abuse and neglect is related to fuller reporting, not an increase in actual occurrences.

This report, Publication No. 20-01099, is available free from the Clearinghouse on Child Abuse and Neglect Information, PO Box 1182, Washington, DC 20013

*   *   *

Report on Children, Youth, and Families

In March 1987, the House Committee on Children, Youth, and Families presented to the One Hundredth Congress a report entitled *Abused Children in America: Victims of Official Neglect*. This 380-page report, compiled largely through a survey of state child protective services agencies in the first half of 1986, attempts to describe the incidence of child maltreatment on a state-by-state basis, the services provided for maltreated children, and the funding available for child protective services. Particularly useful are individual reports on each state which provide the information reported to the survey under the following rubrics: Total Child Abuse and Neglect Reports Received— 1985; Percent of Reports Substantiated; Child Protective Reports by Maltreatment Type; Observed Trends in Child Abuse and Neglect; Factors Contributing to Increase in Reports; Recent Policy Changes; Referrals to and Action by Law Enforcement Officials; Shifts in Staff; Administrative/Policy Barriers to Child Protective and Child Welfare Services; Suggested Allocations of Existing or New Resources; State Initiatives; Prevention and Treatment Approaches; and Administration (which lists addresses, contact persons, and phone numbers).

Conclusions of Report

The conclusions of *Abused Children in America* are as follows:

1) Reports of child abuse, particularly sexual abuse, are on the rise.

2) Reports of child neglect continue to increase.

3) Despite increased reports of child abuse, states are unable to provide needed services.

4) States cite two principal factors leading to increased child abuse reports: increased public awareness and deteriorating economic conditions for families.

5) Prevention is receiving increased attention; states are emphasizing family-based services to prevent unnecessary placement of children out-of-home.

6) Cost-effective programs prevent or reduce child abuse and neglect, strengthen families, and reduce dependency.

7) States lack sufficient law enforcement data and information about how funds for child abuse services were spent.

Minority Dissent

The Republican minority of the House Committee, divided strictly along party lines, offered a dissent to the report, arguing that the data collected by the committee were sometimes misinterpreted and that the reporting was selective. The minority called *Abused Children in America* an advocacy report rather than an objective report. In brief, the dissent stated that the conclusions are blurred by the fact that there is no standard definition among the states of child abuse and neglect, and that laws in many states have changed, affecting the rates of reported maltreatment; that abuse and neglect are confused in the report; that the substantiation percentage is downplayed; that the causes of abuse are not addressed; and that state responses to the committee's survey are subject to the biases of the employee who filled out the report form.

The minority adds its own conclusions:

Minority Conclusions

1) Not enough is being done to strengthen family ties that would prevent child maltreatment.

2) The "most typical" case of maltreatment is neglect, not physical or sexual abuse.

3) "There is good news in terms of Federal and State Responses": Funding levels in constant dollars increased 1.9% between 1981 and 1985.

The minority stated: "Let there be no doubt, however, that we are concerned about the high rates of child abuse and neglect reports. Nor let it be said that we are satisfied with the responses of the public and private sectors to the tragedy of child maltreatment."

Members of the House Select Committee on Children, Youth, and Families in 1987 when *Abused Children in America* was prepared:

DEMOCRATS:
George Miller, CA, Chairman
William Lehman, FL
Patricia Schroeder, CO
Lindy (Mrs. Hale) Boggs, LA
Matthew F. McHugh, NY
Ted Weiss, NY
Beryl Anthony, Jr., AR
Barbara Boxer, CA
Sander M. Levin, MI
Bruce A. Morrison, CO
J. Roy Rowland, GA
Gerry Sikorski, MN
Alan Wheat, MO
Matthew G. Martinez, CA
Lane Evans, IS
Richard J. Durbin, IL
Thomas C. Sawyer, OH
David E. Skaggs, CO

REPUBLICANS:
Dan Coats, IN, Ranking
Minority Member
Thomas J. Bliley, Jr., VA
Frank R. Wolf, VA
Nancy L. Johnson, CT
Barbara F. Vucanovich, NV
Jack F. Kemp, NY
George C. Wortley, NY
Ron Packard, CA
Beau Boulter, TX
J. Dennis Hastert, IL
Clyde C. Holloway, LA
Fred Grandy, IA

As of February 1990, the following changes had taken place on the Select Committee on Children, Youth, and Families.

Democrat Bill Sarpaulius of Texas replaced Thomas C. Sawyer.

Republican Thomas J. Bliley, Jr., of Virginia replaced Dan Coats as Ranking Minority Member.

NEW REPUBLICAN MEMBERS:	THEY REPLACE:
Curt Weldon, PN	Dan Coats
Lamar S. Smith, TX	Nancy L. Johnson
Peter Smith, VT	Jack F. Kemp
James T. Walsh, NY	George C. Wortley
Ronald K. Machtley, RI	Beau Boulter
Tommy F. Robinson, AK	Fred Grandy

Abused Children in America is available free from the Superintendant of documents, U.S. Government Printing Office, Washington D.C. 20402

*   *   *

NCPCA Survey

Since 1985 the National Committee for Prevention of Child Abuse has conducted a telephone survey of child welfare administrators in all 50 states and the District of Columbia and an annual telephone poll to determine public opinion about questions related to child abuse.

Their 1990 survey of child welfare administrators generated responses from 49 administrators who "knew or were able to project their child abuse reporting statistics for 1989" and 41 who had 1989 statistics regarding child abuse fatalities. That survey indicates that 2.4 million reports of child abuse and neglect were filed in 1989 and 1,237 child-abuse related deaths were recorded. Margaret Graham, president of the committee's board of directors concluded, "The most tragic victims of the nation's drug crisis are the nation's children. Confronting this problem with effective prevention services must be our number one priority."

NCPCA Public Opinion Poll

The NCPCA public opinion poll, conducted by telephone, surveys 1,250 randomly selected adults nationwide, asking such questions as "How often do you think physical punishment of a child leads to injury of the child?" and "Have you done anything personally to prevent child abuse in the past year?" The committee concluded from the 1990 poll that there seems to have been "a shift in public perception and parental practices with respect to the use of physical punishment and verbal abuse. . ." Today parents appear significantly less inclined to use corporal punishment and a greater percentage of the general public perceives this behavior damaging. While public opinion has consistently questioned the repeated yelling and swearing at a child, parental practices are begining to reflect this public perception.

"A sizable percentage of the public remains optimistic about their ability to make a difference in the child abuse problem. A sizable percent of the public is involved in such diverse activities as talking to a parent to try to stop abuse, offering assistance to a parent under stress, and providing financial support to an organization working to prevent child abuse."

Information about the 1990 Survey and Public Opinion Poll is available free from the National Committee for the Prevention of Child Abuse, Post Office Box 2866, Chicago, IL. 60690

Perspective: Making the Public Aware

Joy Byers

*Joy L. Byers is Director of Public Awareness and Information for
the National Committee for Prevention of Child Abuse
(NCPCA), which was founded in 1972 by Chicago philanthro-
pist Donna J. Stone. The NCPCA is now represented throughout
the country by sixty-seven chapters, with at least one in each
state. Its mission is a nationwide commitment to preventing
child abuse in all its forms, and with that aim it devotes a great
deal of time and money to promoting public awareness of child
abuse. The NCPCA is a nonprofit organization funded by corpo-
rate and individual donations and by the sale of its own publications.*

CI: When you talk about public awareness, are you referring to
education as well?

**Public
Education**

BYERS: I mean public education in several ways. We educate
through our publications, and we also have a national media
campaign for which our Public Awareness and Information
Department provides television spots, radio spots, and print
materials. We work through the Advertising Council of New
York to develop that campaign.

CI: You also do an annual national study of child abuse and
neglect reporting. How is your study conducted, and what does
it concentrate on?

**National
Research
Center**

BYERS: Through the National Research Center based here at
NCPCA, we have since 1985 done a yearly survey of all the
departments of human services throughout the country. We
study the numbers of reports that have been made through
those departments and track whether the reports are going up
or down; we track numbers of fatalities from each state due to
child abuse—we're particularly interested in that; and we also
look at the different types of abuse. We find out from the states

too what their case load looks like: for instance, whether emotional abuse is a big issue and whether alcohol and drug abuse happens to be a big issue in a lot of the reports. We're interested in that kind of information as well.

CI: How does your study compare with the American Humane Association report?

BYERS: The American Humane report was done in somewhat more detail than ours. Our report is limited to fairly basic information. We don't break down everything. For instance, I couldn't tell you from our latest statistics how many teenagers were involved in abuse, or how many children under the age of five. We look at the bigger picture.

Comparison of Surveys

CI: The Department of Health and Human Services funded the American Humane Association report, which I understand was done as a requirement of federal legislation mandating a report. Are you taking on that function now in their place?

BYERS: No. Our study doesn't take the place of that. We've always done it on our own, just as part of what we do; we don't get funding for it. My understanding is that the gathering of that data was put out for bid, and Walter McDonald & Associates from Sacramento, California, will now be doing what AHA was doing. It's not a competition as far as we are concerned.

CI: What does your 1989 study show?

BYERS: It shows that reports of child abuse cases have gone up some, not dramatically: our figure shows about 2.4 million. And the total projected fatalities nationwide is over 1,200.

1989 Report

CI: So that's not a dramatic rise either.

BYERS: It's not dramatic, but we're still seeing probably three children a day in this country who are dying from abuse, so it's a major concern. And then again we know that that's a very conservative figure, because it depends on how a state determines whether or not a child has died from abuse, and there's nothing standardized in the way states keep their statistics.

CI: What seems remarkable in the study you just completed? Do you see any red flags, any warnings about things going badly or causes for new concern?

BYERS: I think the most notable fact from the study is the large numbers of cases that involve substance abuse. That's the red flag right now, and I think that is going to impact the field for

Notable Changes

years to come.

CI: Do you break substance abuse down? Do you mean alcohol or drugs or crack cocaine?

Substance Abuse and Child Abuse

BYERS: We're looking particularly at the crack cocaine problem with the numbers of people who are involved in that and the numbers of babies being born addicted to the drug. Tied in with that are high levels of family violence. They all seem to go hand in hand. In the past we might have seen a father who had been a heroin user, but at least the mother was there to keep some kind of stability in the family, because most women didn't get involved in heroin. Now, with the prevalence of crack cocaine, which women are using as well, chaos seems to rule these homes. There's no one there to protect the children, so they're tragic victims of the whole drug crisis.

CI: Having taken the first step, which is describing the problem, how now do you deal with it?

Developing Programs

BYERS: I think we need to encourage more programs that would be available throughout the local communities. We know that in many cases programs are not available to those who need them. For instance, if a substance abuser is already pregnant, she cannot get into a program. Or people may be put on a waiting list for a severe substance abuse program. You have to wonder what the chances are that they will actually be around when their number comes up. It's a tough problem, and it's one that I don't think a lot of people probably predicted would be the most impactful issue happening right now. I think the major challenge is mobilizing the concern people have into efforts to establish programs that ultimately will prevent mistreatment of children, and also maybe get the adults back on track.

CI: Do you think there's sufficient cooperation between the activists in the field of child abuse and neglect and those people involved in the so-called drug war?

BYERS: Yes. I think there's a lot of cooperation, a lot of concern.

CI: Do you see a correlation between the ages of children (ages considered difficult, for example, such as under two or three, when children can't speak) and the incidence of abuse?

Vulnerable Age

BYERS: The most extreme cases tend to be the youngest children, and fatalities too will be children under five. But what's causing that wouldn't necessarily be what's going on with the children but rather the presence of conditions such as extreme poverty and drug use, or if you have other kinds of violence going on in the home.

CI: The second National Incidence Study indicated that roughly half of the occurrences of child maltreatment that were known to professionals working with children, such as teachers, were not reported to CPS. What do you make of that trend?

BYERS: I don't know how one would determine that. What we're seeing, based on a public attitudes study, is that people are much more willing and more likely to report now than in the past. I think most professionals now know that they are mandated by law to report cases when they suspect them.

CI: As I understood the conclusions of the National Incidence Study, the feeling was that people lacked faith in the CPS response to reports.

BYERS: I think most people in the field are aware that CPS workers are overwhelmed with their caseloads. They are having to be responsible for far too many cases. It's impossible for them to keep up with the case loads they have, and the numbers keep going up. They're not getting the support they need to keep up. The funding isn't keeping pace with the numbers of reports that are made every year.

CPS Workload

CI: Do you think CPS response is adequate given the resources they have to deal with?

BYERS: We're seeing that they are more willing maybe than ever before to deal with the cases they have, because certainly they come under fire when there is a fatality or a child is severely damaged. I think they are criticized so much that they try to do the best they can, but they're terribly handicapped by the lack of funds and lack of staff to cover their case loads. I think too that they're seeing more serious cases now with drugs being an issue, and you see cases where children are placed back in homes they've been abused in, for lack of resources.

CPS Response

CI: So the boundaries of social workers' responsibilities are always being redefined; they're given more responsibility every year.

BYERS: Yes. I think they're under a great deal of pressure, and they certainly don't make the news when something good happens, but only when there's a horrendous case that we all read about, like Lisa Steinberg. Everybody knows that case and everybody knows that family. Social workers certainly do some

CPS Unheralded

very good things and probably prevent children from being further abused than they are, but we never hear about that.

CI: Do you see any conclusions that are indicated by the low rate of case substantiation by CPS? We tend to get substantiation statistics, but not unfounded, unsubstantiated statistics; so it's difficult to know how many cases are simply filed away without a determination having been made.

Verifying Reports

BYERS: Again I think that goes back to the lack of continuity between the states. As part of our study, we did track substantiation rates. They vary widely from state to state. This is partly because some states accept any reports that come in; their substantiation rate is going to be very low. Obviously when states are more selective in what they will take as a report, the substantiation rate is higher.

CI: Education, you said, is one way to go about preventing abuse and neglect. How else does one go about it?

Education

BYERS: Education is the key, I think. We've seen dramatic increases in public awareness. Back in 1977, when we were about to launch our first national media campaign, we did a Louis Harris poll to determine what the level of public awareness was on child abuse and how serious a problem the public thought it was. We came up with a level of ten percent awareness among the people who were polled—that is, ten percent of those people thought child abuse was indeed a serious problem in this country. In 1983 the poll was redone, after several years of our national media campaign and also the work of other organizations who were by then involved in educating people as well. That poll showed that the awareness rate had gone to a ninety percent level. So obviously we believe very much in doing everything that can be done to educate the public. That's the first step: making them aware that there is a problem. The next thing you can do, of course, is to change behavior. That's the more difficult step.

CI: How do you go about doing that?

NCPCA Programs

BYERS: We here at NCPCA again fall back on our media campaign. Currently we have a campaign on verbal abuse of children, because we feel that as a form of emotional abuse, it can do every bit as much damage as physical abuse can do. Since 1987 we have been trying to bombard the public, if you will, with messages about verbal abuse. We're saying, "Words can hit as hard as a fist. Stop using words that hurt. Start using words that help." What that does is make people aware of how it feels from a child's point of view to be constantly torn apart verbally by a parent. We include our post office box number in all our media campaign material, and we get hundreds of pieces of mail. A lot of them are from parents who say, "I heard myself on television. I saw myself. That's what I do. I never thought of it as abuse." That's simply the case, that people don't see it as abuse. Once we make them aware, I think they're much more likely to take a look at their behavior and say, "Well, maybe this isn't the way."

CI: How much stock do you put in the premise that parents who were physically punished as children are likely to punish their own children the same way?

BYERS: I've heard an awful lot of parents say, "I was spanked as a kid, and it never hurt me." I think it's a natural reaction to repeat the kind of behavior that your parents used, because we learn to parent by the way we were parented. If I had been spanked routinely as a child, I would guess that most people dealt with their children that way unless I was educated on a change in public attitudes about the way we deal with children.

Abused Parents

CI: Is there much hope of identifying potentially abusive people so that preventive treatment can be offered?

BYERS: Self-help groups can be useful in that way.   Most people really have the sense that things aren't going right. They know. But there's still a certain stigma attached to admitting you need help. It's always tough to ask for help, for some reason—we feel we should be able to do everything on our own. If we identify people as high-risk people from the beginning, maybe in the hospital when a baby is born and the staff sees some behaviors from the mother or the father that don't look encouraging, recommendations can be made to them and some community support offered to get them on track—hopefully before abusive behavior occurs. But sometimes that doesn't happen until they're already in the system.

Abuser Treatment

CI: Do you have any sense of the differences in attitudes toward maltreatment in the United States as compared to other developed countries?

BYERS: We are one of the last of the developed countries to ban corporal punishment in our schools. I think that says a lot about us in terms of teaching children that the way to have authority or power and the way to solve problems is by hitting. We have

Attitudes in the U.S.

a strange attitude about that; on the one hand, we're seen as very open, friendly people who are not out to hurt others, and yet we see nothing wrong with spanking children in the schools, where we would like for them to feel safe and protected. That seems to be something of a double standard. Even England several years ago banned corporal punishment. We're on our way here, but we still have a majority of states that allow physical punishment in schools.

CI: Certainly it would be hard to deny that American society is one of the most violent among what we call the developed nations, and I suppose that attitude has to spill over into the way people treat children.

Violence in Society

BYERS: My guess, though, is that the average person here would not want to be thought of as part of a violent society. I think that we tend to think of ourselves as above that sort of behavior and attitude; and yet it's very obvious from the number of people who feel it's OK to hit children that there is a certain amount of acceptance of it.

CI: Are there reasons to feel encouraged?

Gains

BYERS: One thing I'm very encouraged about is that since we began our campaign in 1987 on verbal abuse, we're now seeing, according to our poll, that fifteen percent fewer parents are using yelling and swearing at children as a method of discipline. I think that makes a statement about the power of educating people through the media. That's gratifying. For the last year, our polls show that sixty percent of the parents who were surveyed said they hadn't yelled or sworn at their children, and forty percent said they never used spanking or hitting. So I think we're making headway. I think we're on the right track. We just have to keep at it and not let up.

4

Characteristics of the Abused Child

On July 7, 1962, a seven-page article called "The Battered-Child Syndrome" by two pediatricians (Dr. C. Henry Kempe and Dr. Henry K. Silver), a gynecologist (Dr. William Droegemueller), a psychiatrist (Dr. Brandt F. Steele), and a radiologist (Dr. Frederic N. Silverman) was published in the *Journal of the American Medical Association.* That article, written under the generalship of Dr. Kempe, marks the beginning of the public awareness of child abuse and neglect as defined in the previous chapter. Dr. Kempe, Chairman of the Department of Pediatrics at the University of Colorado School of Medicine, and his staff had been studying patterns of abuse in their patients since 1951, and they had concluded convincingly that physical abuse of young children was a "frequent cause of permanent injury or death." Dr. Kempe had recently written a letter to more than three hundred district attorneys advising them of this problem, and he was directly responsible for alerting the U.S. Congress to the need for governmental responses.

"The Battered Child"

In gathering material for their article, Dr. Kempe and his colleagues undertook a nationwide survey of seventy-one hospitals, which confirmed their own observations. The Battered Child Syndrome, more fully explored in *The Battered Child*, edited by Dr. Kempe and Dr. Ray E. Helfer (1968, revised 1972, further revised 1980), was described as "a clinical condition in young children who have received serious physical abuse, generally from a parent or a foster parent." The victim was described as usually under the age of three, as usually displaying signs of neglect as well as physical abuse, and as usually being the victim of repeated attacks. The parent-abuser was described as often being psychotic and of low intelligence, "immature, impulsive, self-centered, hypersensitive, and quick to react with poorly controlled agression." Frequently the parent had himself been the victim of abuse. But Dr. Kempe and his associates were careful to point out that not all abusers fall into the same

Research

categories of socioeconomic status and psychotic behavior: "It also occurs among people with good education and stable financial and social background. However, from the scant data that are available, it would appear that in these cases, too, there is a defect in character structure which allows aggressive impulses to be expressed too freely. There is also some suggestion that the attacking parent was subjected to similar abuse in childhood."

Professional Appeal
The authors of "The Battered-Child Syndrome" challenged physicians to report child maltreatment when they observed it, or suspected they had, for the sole purpose of preventing abusive treatment from recurring. They laid out the rationale for the governmental response to child abuse which has prevailed since—treatment, not punishment; attention to the child's welfare above all other considerations, even if the child must be removed from the home. "The bias should be in favor of the child's safety: everything should be done to prevent repeated trauma, and the physician should not be satisfied to return the child to an environment where even a moderate risk of repetition exists."

Legislation
Within five years of the publication of "The Battered-Child Syndrome" every state had adopted legislation addressing the issue of child abuse and neglect, and by 1980 forty-eight states had adopted laws requiring certain people to report abuse or suspected abuse to CPS, law enforcement agencies, or both. An important feature of federal legislation on the mistreatment of children is the requirement to study the problem. That is why we have available such full and ambitious reports of incidence and demographics of abusers and the abused. Federal funding has also stimulated the study of abuse and neglect victims to determine indicators, both physical and behavioral, of their predicament.

Caution
Indicator lists should always be used with caution. It is possible (though unlikely) for a child to show coincidentally many of the symptoms of a type of abuse or neglect. The symptoms do not necessarily prove incidence; they are good clues, however.

Duty to Report
Several groups have prepared lists of symptoms of abuse or neglect. The one presented here is circulated by the Children's Safety Project in Manhattan. Not every child victim displays all or even most of the indicators listed here, and other indicators may be present. If one suspects maltreatment, he or she should report the case immediately to the appropriate authority,

usually the department of social services. A maltreated child—as well as the maltreater—needs the help of a trained therapist, physician, or social worker. A list of agencies designated in each state to receive reports, and information on how to contact them, is listed on pp. 89-94.

PHYSICAL ABUSE

Physical Indicators

Behavioral Indicators

Unexplained bruises or welts; may be in various stages of healing, or in clusters of unusual patterns, or on several different areas

Unexplained burns; in shape of cigarette, rope, or iron or caused by immersion which may appear sock- or glovelike

Unexplained lacerations to mouth, lips, arms, legs, or torso

Unexplained skeletal injuries or stiff swollen joints, or multiple or spiral fractures

Missing or loosened teeth

Human bite marks

Bald spots

Unexplained abrasions

Appearance of injuries after school absence, weekend, or vacation

Easily frightened or fearful of adults/parents, or of physical contact, or when other children cry

Destructive to self and/or others

Extremes of behavior: aggressive, withdrawn

Poor social relations

Learning problems; poor academic performance, short attention span, language delayed

Runaway or delinquent behavior

Reporting unbelievable reasons for injuries

Complaints of soreness or moves awkwardly

Accident prone

Wears clothing that clearly is meant to cover body when not appropriate

Seems afraid to go home

SEXUAL ABUSE

Physical Indicators	Behavioral Indicators
Difficulty walking/sitting	Sudden radical behavior change
Torn, stained, or bloody underclothing	Destructive to self and/or others
Genital/anal itching, pain, swelling, burning	Extremes in behavior: aggressive, withdrawn
Genital/anal bruises or bleeding	Poor social relations
Frequent urinary tract or yeast infections	Refuses to change for gym
Pain on urination	Behaves seductively and has sexual knowledge beyond age
Vaginal/penile discharge	Sexually acts out or attempts to force or coerce other children to be sexual
Poor sphincter control	
Venereal disease	Regressive behavior
Pregnancy	Runaway or delinquent behavior
Chronic unexplained sore throats	Complains of soreness or moves or sits awkwardly
Frequent psychosomatic illnesses	Wears clothing that covers body when not appropriate
Loss of appetite	Depressed/apathetic or suicidal
	Compulsive bathing
	Nightmares

NEGLECT

Physical Indicators	Behavioral Indicators
Poor growth pattern	Developmental lags
Constant hunger	Begs or steals food, forages through garbage
Malnutrition	
	Always hungry
Poor hygiene: body odor, lice	Destructive to self and/or others
Inappropriate clothing	
	Extremes in behavior: aggressive, withdrawn
Constant fatigue	
Listlessness	Hyperactive
Falls asleep in school	Assumes adult responsibilities or acts in pseudo-mature fashion
Consistent lack of supervision; especially for long periods or in dangerous activities	
	Exhibits infantile behavior
Unexplained bruises or injuries as a result of poor supervision	Delinquent behavior
	Depressed/apathetic; states "no one cares"
Unattended physical problems or medical needs such as: -lack of proper immunizations -gross dental problems -needs glasses/hearing aids	Frequent school absences or chronic tardiness
	Seeks attention and/or affection
	Hypochondria

EMOTIONAL MALTREATMENT

Physical Indicators

Failure to thrive

Developmental lags

Wetting of bed/pants

Thumbsucking

Appears sad

Speech disorders

Health problems:
 -ulcers
 -asthma
 -skin disorders
 -severe allergies
 -obesity
 -extreme weight loss

Poor appearance

Drug or alcohol abuse

Behavioral Indicators

Habit disorders: sucking, biting, rocking, etc.

Destructive to self and/or others

Extremes in behavior: aggressive, withdrawn

Phobias, sleep disorders, etc.

Developmental lags: mental, emotional

Learning problems

Inhibition of play

Cruelty, vandalism, stealing, cheating, etc.

Overly adaptive behavior:
 -inappropriately adult
 -inappropriately infantile

Depression

Suicidal ideation

Perspective: Treating Victims and Their Families

Flora Colao

Flora Colao is among the leading child therapists in the United States. Since graduating from Adelphi University with a master's degree in social work, she has set up model programs for the treatment of abused women, abused children, and their families. A native New Yorker, she developed the rape crisis program at St. Vincent's Hospital and the Children's Safety Project in Manhattan, which she founded and directs. She has served as a consultant to the FBI task force on sexually exploited children and to state and local child protective services agencies throughout the country. Along with martial arts specialist Tamar Hosansky, Ms. Colao wrote Your Children Should Know: Personal-Safety Strategies for Parents to Teach Their Children *(Indianapolis: Bobbs-Merrill, 1983; reprinted in paperback by Perennial Library, 1987), and the materials in that book were used by the authors and collaborators to develop the Children's Personal Safety Kit™, an educational resource package.*

CI: What is the Children's Safety Project?

COLAO: It is a program that is designed to deal with both prevention and aftercare in relation to child abuse. We offer children personal safety classes where they learn crime avoidance and self-defense that is appropriate to their age, size, speed, and the environment they live in. We also teach children very specifically what abuse is—what kinds of abuse there are and what kinds of risk they face depending on their age. For example, if we're doing a class for preschool children, we teach that you own your body and what you do if you get lost in a store, environmentally accurate things that a preschool child would be dealing with. If we're dealing with teenagers, we would address issues relating to them: how they should behave on their own; how people might trick them or get them into a compromising situation; what would happen if they decided to

Children's Safety Project

experiment with drugs or alcohol—how that compromises their personal safety. We also teach physical resistance they can use if they're confronted with a threatening situation.

CI: Do you deal with both abuse and neglect?

COLAO: Yes.

CI: And all types, I assume?

Children's View of Child Abuse and Neglect

COLAO: Absolutely. We deal with physical, sexual, and emotional abuse as well as neglect. And we try to maintain a child's perspective on those issues. When we talk with children, we ask them, "What do you think physical abuse is?" "Are parents allowed to hit children?" "Are grownups allowed to hit children?" When they say "Yes," we ask, "When does it become abuse?"

CI: In your therapy programs, do you find yourself altering the definition of abuse as a result of that approach?

COLAO: I find that we arrive at a much more accurate definition. In our printed material, we compare the standard definition of abuse with children's definitions. It is much more accurate to ask children for the definition. If you ask a child when is it that words hurt you, you get answers like "Well, that's when your mother says she wishes she had an abortion." That's a very accurate description of emotional abuse. What is sexual abuse? "Well, that's when they want to teach you how to do sex." That is a very accurate description from a seven-year-old. When we're dealing with personal safety and crime avoidance, we try to learn from the case histories that we have and look at what may have helped those children in that situation. We are careful not to blame the child for not having known how to deal with it.

CI: How big is the Children's Safety Project? How many clients do you have; how many staff members?

COLAO: There is me; I'm the director. I have an administrator who has been donated to me for a year and who is there three days a week, sometimes four.

CI: When you say donated, do you mean private funds or public?

Personal Safety Classes

COLAO: Private funds. And then, due to a small grant from the state, we have five additional consultants, including an art therapist, a social worker, a counseling student, and two self-defense instructors who also have some counseling experience. Everybody sort of switches off as needed. The personal safety classes are both for children who we know have been abused and for children who are considered at risk for abuse—maybe they have been identified by social agencies as being at risk. The classes also include children whose parents or families are simply concerned that they learn prevention. So it is a mixed group. In any given class, about half the kids have already had some abusive experience or someone very close to them has. We also have a lot of children who are simply identified as so-called problem children—who are acting out and nobody really knows what's wrong, but they know something's up with this kid. Sometimes we uncover abuse, and sometimes we really don't know what's going on; but we know there's something, and this is an outlet for them.

Art Expression Group

We also have an art-expression therapy group, which originated because we were seeing a number of sibling pairs in which one child had been abused and the other hadn't. What was happening was that it seemed to the child who had not been abused that the abused was getting rewarded; that the identified victim, for lack of a better term, was getting a lot of services, and the child who wasn't abused wasn't getting anything, or at least it seemed that way to the child. So we started the group to work with children in that situation, to work with sibling pairs, so we could sort of equalize the treatment in the nonabused child's eyes: "You're coming to the same group; she is not or he is not going to a special group; you're coming together." This program is also for children who have a difficult time being verbally expressive. A lot of the kids who are identified as school problems are simply learning-disabled children who have difficulty with written or verbal skills but happen to do very well in a nonverbal, very free kind of situation. They do well with art as a means of expressing their feelings.

CI: Do you have a formal relationship with child protective services?

COLAO: No. Not in relation to the Children's Safety Project.

CI: Are there other programs similar to the Children's Safety Project?

Self-defense Training

COLAO: I am not aware of any that do both prevention and aftercare. There are preventive services programs that have counseling for families in which it is known or suspected that there has been abuse. There are a lot of aftercare programs that have funding specifically for court-mandated treatment. I don't know of any programs that are doing both, and I don't know of any that have a physical component. We build in self-defense training as part of our treatment, and also as part of an individual's counseling there is the option of putting the child in an office we have set up that has targets to beat into or to yell at or to kick or do whatever he or she needs to do—a place where nobody is going to say shut up; sit down; you're bad; keep quiet; or anything like that. They have a physical outlet for their emotional pain, because any kind of abuse has both a physical and an emotional component.

CI: Your treatment has to deal primarily with the emotional component of abuse, using a physical outlet to deal with it.

COLAO: The child should feel that the whole self is being dealt with. I've found in my work with children that if you give them permission to get rid of their physical aggression in a controlled setting—like the safety classes or the office where they can hit a target or even helping the parents set up a tantrum corner—then it is easier for them to control their aggression in other situations because they have learned that this is an appropriate outlet for aggressions and there are other inappropriate outlets.

CI: Is any part of your program aimed at parents, particularly nonabusive parents of abused children?

Programs for Parents COLAO: Absolutely, as often as the staff is able we have parents in workshops. We are currently setting up a series of workshops for foster parents. One of the workshops we're offering for them is in recognizing the signs and symptoms of child abuse. Sometimes a child is placed in a foster home for neglect but in fact has a history of abuse that has gone unrecognized. We are offering a workshop on disciplining the abused child, because, as far as I'm concerned, the worst form of discipline you can use with an abused child is corporal punishment. An abused child is often very physically aggressive and provocative and very difficult to discipline. We also work with nonoffending parents on the same issues. In some cases I'll bring the parents into the session. For example, I'm working with two preschool children who were abused in a child-care setting. They are three-and-a-half and four-and-a-half. The abuse was only recently discovered, and it didn't come from their disclosure; it came from the disclosure of another child who had gone to the same child-care center. The parents of my clients realized that their children had acted out when they were at the child-care center and seemed to be calmer since they had left. So the parents asked their children if they had been abused and they said yes. I bring the parents into that session to work together. I talk to them about why their children might need a physical outlet to deal with what is going on and show the parents how I do that with their kids. That way they can set up a similar outlet at home.

CI: In reading your book I was surprised to find that one of the major difficulties a sexually abused child faces is the lack of support from nonoffending family members, either before or after the act.

COLAO: It is so difficult for many parents, first to believe that this could happen; second to face it; and third to deal with their own feelings about it. So it's much easier to deny—or to say she seems fine or she's doing well—than to deal with the knowledge that the child is still hurting and the hurt comes up in different ways at different times. Parents would be much happier to say she's just being obstinate or she's just being a brat than to believe the thing that happened two years ago is still bothering her, because they may feel like failures as parents: "I didn't do the right thing; I didn't figure out the right way to help him or her through this; or I must have been a bad parent because my child didn't come to me as soon as this happened."

Support for Sexually Abused Children

CI: Do you find that generally speaking boys and girls differ in their responses as victims?

COLAO: Absolutely. Boys take longer to disclose than girls—and girls take a long time—for one thing. Boys think they should have been able to handle the situation, that it is a reflection of their masculinity or lack of masculinity that they didn't know what to do, that they didn't fight. They worry that people will think they are homosexual—whether or not it was a male who abused them. I've had boys abused by females who worry that because they didn't like what happened they must be gay because boys are supposed to like that stuff. Boys who have been abused by men say, "Well, if I tell people that I did something sexual with a man then they're gonna say I'm gay." So they lose either way. I find that much less so with girls. I do see some girls who wonder about their sexuality, but much less so than with boys. I also see a higher level of suicidal ideation with boys than with girls, and, I think, a much higher level of destructiveness than with girls in terms of acting-out behavior

Different Responses of Boys and Girls to Abuse

that gets them into trouble. Many more boys end up labeled juvenile delinquents than girls. Aggression is more acceptable in males. In some cases aggression is the way boys react to abuse.

CI: Are there certain types of kids who are more likely to be abused than others, either as a result of certain behavioral patterns that they've adopted or because of environmental conditions?

Profile of Victim

COLAO: Both. Children who are raised to obey and respond unquestioningly to authority figures are at great risk, because they will do as they are told: "For the simple reason that so and so told me." Even when they are confronted by someone abusing authority, they don't see that they have any way out because they've been raised to be good and to obey. These children are at great risk.

Children who are in environments where they are not supervised or where they are neglected or where they are treated as unimportant are at great risk, first of all of being befriended by pedophiles, or of just being accessible to people who will abuse them. The child presumes that there is something about him that brought it on. You have a child who is emotionally or physically abused at home, and then you have somebody who is offering him friendship. The child thinks he has to exchange sex for friendship because he doesn't feel he is worth anything more. That comes up often. Kids say to me that they don't understand why everybody is making a fuss about sexual abuse. I have one little girl who says to me, "Why is everybody so upset about that? That's when he told me he loved me. Nobody cared when he was pulling my hair." From her perspective it was ludicrous that we were concerned about the sex. As far as she was concerned nobody cared when he pulled her hair; nobody cared when he punched her; but everybody cared when he was tickling her vagina. That doesn't make sense to her.

CI: Authorities in the field say abusers tend to have been abused themselves. Does this agree with your experience?

Abusers Who Were Victims

COLAO: I have limited experience with abusers, because I only see the ones that are really highly motivated for treatment; but among the children that I've seen who have abused other children, every one has a history of abuse, usually quite severe abuse. Often referrals come to me because a child is abusive towards other children. You might have, for example, a twelve-year-old who sexually abused a four-year-old. When you look at his history or her history there has usually been severe abuse in that background.

CI: Are there other identifiers?

COLAO: That's certainly one. Usually there was no outlet for them.

CI: What do you mean by outlet?

COLAO: They had no other way, as far as they could tell, of having any sense of control in their lives. These children who have abused other children felt that the only way they could have some sense of control over their feelings was by doing to someone else what was done to them. Sometimes they started abusing other children as a way to get help. I had one kid who said, "Well, when he did it to me they got him a therapist." As far as he could tell, that was the only way you could get a therapist. In this case, he was sexually abused at age five by a sixteen-year-old. When he was about ten he started asking for help; he started to say that he was feeling crazy. No one had ever dealt with what had happened to him. The advice had been "he'll forget it." Basically no attention was paid to him, so when he was twelve, he sexually abused a four-year-old neighbor. And then, magically, everybody was referring him for treatment to find out what was wrong with him. As far as he could tell, that was the way you got a therapist.

Victims and the Need for Treatment

CI: There's been a public discussion lately about whether molesters themselves can be rehabilitated. These fourteen-, fifteen-, sixteen- year-old kids who have, maybe as a result of their own abuse, begun abusing others: Are they lost causes?

COLAO: If you've caught them early they're not. And if they have not become compulsive they're not. My experience with kids who have abused other children is that if they were caught the first time or very close to the first time, it's very easy and it's not a lot of work to get them to learn how to control their behavior and not to reoffend. But the children who have been doing this for years and nobody has paid attention or have been doing this for years and gotten away with it have likely become compulsive, and their behavior has become linked to so many other things that they are very difficult to treat. There is controversy in the field as to how "rehabilitatable" they are.

Treating Abusers

CI: Do you prepare children to testify in court?

COLAO: All the time.

CI: That must be a demanding responsibility.

**Victims'
Testimony**

COLAO: It is. Actually, I think in some ways it is easier than other parts of my job. My experience with children in court is that if they're properly prepared, court can be quite a resolution for them. It can offer them the opportunity to get closure on the experience; it can offer them the opportunity to feel empowered over what happened to them; and it can offer them the opportunity to say, "OK. I fought back, and I can be sure he's not going to do this or she's not going to do this to me again, or to anybody else." What needs to be addressed is court from the child's perspective: "What are you scared of? What do you think is going to happen?" A lot of times children think that the abuser is going to be allowed to do something to them in court. That they're going to be sent to jail if they make a mistake, or if they don't remember something. So the job is really to prepare them accurately for what's going to happen. Often you can turn around what the child is afraid of and give him or her a sense of power over it.

I've had children say to me, "Oh, I'll be so scared to see him"; or "I'll be so scared to see her"; and I'll say, "Yeah, it is scary. It's very scary to go to court. Absolutely. But you know what? He's a lot more scared of you." That's new information: "What do you mean?" "Well, he knows he can go to jail for what he did. He can go to jail. All you have to do is tell the truth." I'll have kids say to me, "I'll be so embarrassed," or "I'll be so ashamed." "Well what are you ashamed of?" "I'm ashamed of all those things that happened." "Well think about how ashamed he'll be. He's gonna have to sit there while you tell on him, and everybody's gonna say how could he do that to such a nice little boy or such a nice little girl." You have to turn the experience around. When I work with children who start acting out and are very difficult or who have been labeled bad children, one of the things that I tell the parents or the teachers or anybody working with them is that it is time to reverse their identity. The child is assuming "I'm bad and here's all this proof that I'm bad. I'm so bad that this happened to me. I'm so bad that I'm acting out in school. I'm so bad I'm getting punished." So one of the things that I do first is I say, "I know you're good. I know you're good inside. What I don't understand is why you keep doing all these things to try to convince everybody that you're bad." So the internal identity becomes that of the good child. It's not the bad child waiting to be discovered, it's the good child that nobody has recognized, who's stuck inside and really scared. You reverse the sense of the split and then it's much easier to start getting the behavior under control.

CI: Do you have any comments to offer on handling of child witnesses in the McMartin case in California in which widespread sexual abuse at a day-care center was alleged?

McMartin Case

COLAO: First of all, it was so long. It was just so long that everyone involved had to wait. It was really too much. I think that we've all learned a lot in the last six and a half years. We can all take any one of those interviews and say you should have done this; you should have done that; you should have done the other thing. But six years ago interviewing children for criminal proceedings was a brand new field. I really don't think it would be fair to critique the interviewers at this point. I think that we can all look and say we've learned a lot and identify the things we need to pay attention to. You know, investigative interviewing is different from therapeutic interviewing. To give you an example, if I'm working with a five-year-old child when I'm not part of the investigation, and I'm not worried about whether I have to testify in court or whether the child has to testify in court, and I say tell me what happened, he might say, "Well, you know they did this to me and they did that"; and then he says, "Then I turned into Superman and I flied out of the room." Ok. If I'm looking at that case therapeutically. I might explore that fantasy a little bit more. I might say, "Well, how does it feel to be Superman?" I might say, "What made you turn into Superman?" I might explore the fantasy a lot more because therapeutically that may have been the fantasy that got him through what happened to him. But if I'm part of the investigative team, or if I have to worry about him going to court, then I might say, "Wait a minute, let's talk about what really happened. I know you couldn't turn into Superman and fly out of the room, so let's talk about what really happened." Those are very different things, and I think that one of the things that happened in the McMartin case is when Kee MacFarlane was originally doing the interviews she was doing them from the perspective of a therapist as opposed to that of an investigator who is part of the prosecution.

CI: How often have you encountered children whom you believed to be fantasizing abuse, particularly sexual abuse?

**Fantasy
and Sexual
Abuse**

COLAO: My experience is that children don't fantasize sexual abuse or physical abuse. They will, however, outright lie about it. I deal with false allegations. Children who make false allegations do it for a variety of reasons. One is that they may feel they have to at the request of someone else. It's very seldom child generated; it's usually generated to please an adult—sometimes a parent, sometimes another relative. Sometimes it's because they think a lie is going to protect a parent. To give you an example, I worked with a child whose mother was battered. The child falsely alleged that her stepfather was sexually abusing her because she knew it would get her mother out of the situation. She had a very clear means to an end, as far as she could tell, and she knew enough about the way the system worked to know that they would either force the stepfather out or take her out and put her mother in the position of choosing between her and the stepfather. She felt pretty confident that her mother would choose her. It was very clear to her that this accusation was going to get her mother out of this miserable situation, which her mother did not have the strength to leave on her own. I had another child who accused her stepfather because she wanted her mother and father back together, and she felt if she accused her stepfather that her mother would throw him out and then there was a chance of her mother and father reconciling. There are sometimes very clear results that the child is looking for. Sometimes in the case of allegations I've found to be false, it has really been a case of misinterpretation by a well-meaning adult.

**False
Assumptions
and Malice**

To give you an example, you have a mother who herself had a history of being sexually abused as a child, and her child comes home and says, "I don't like Mr. so and so the bus driver." "Why?" "He's always bothering me." Mom says, "That's what I used to say when this was happening to me!" And suddenly there's an accusation against the school bus driver based on the word of this child. The mother presents the child-reported sexual abuse, and everybody investigates it as if the child had actually reported sexual abuse. I had one situation where the child reported being annoyed that her father was tickling her between her legs. Immediately everybody assumed sexual abuse; they wanted to remove the child. I sat down with her and asked what do you mean. I didn't make any assumptions. It turned out that he was tickling her just above the knee. The misunderstanding came from the adults being uncomfortable asking for details of what she meant and assuming that when a child says "between my legs" she means the same thing adults mean. Then there are the children who absolutely feel forced to make an allegation against someone because they've been told to. I wish there weren't malicious adults but there are. Sometimes it's divorce cases; sometimes it's other difficulties that people are having. I don't think it occurs in as many divorce cases as people think, but yes, it certainly does happen in divorce cases. But there are malicious adults: "I'll get you, and you'll be sorry," and then they tell. I know of a landlord-tenant dispute in which a four-year-old felt like she had to do what mom said. But those kinds of situations often require a minimum of investigation before the truth comes out.

Then there are the children who have witnessed abuse against others and who present with very similar symptoms; everybody keeps saying rule out sexual abuse. To give you an example, I had a child who was not quite six years old, knocking down little girls in a kindergarten class, pulling up their dresses and jumping on them. "What are you doing?" "I'm humping them." Everybody was saying, "Is he sexually abused? He must be sexually abused." And this went on. They would ask him, and he would say no. But everybody was convinced. He's just not telling us; he was really abused. Well, I sat down with him and said, "I heard that when you're at school you're knocking down these little girls, and you're humping them." He looked at me with an expression on his face like the cat who got the canary. He didn't answer, and I said, "Well, I just want to know where you learned about that." He said, "Oh, that's about nasty stuff." I said, "OK, I'll make a deal with you. I'm not going to be angry at you. I'm not going to think you're bad. I'm not going to tell anybody else about it until we talk and I tell you who I'm going to tell and why. Can you tell me where you learned it? And when?" He proceeded to describe witnessing his mother being raped, on numerous occasions. "And what did mommy do?" I asked. "Mommy cried, 'Oh God! Somebody please help me!'" And he didn't know what to do. So I said, "And what happens when you do it at school?" "They pick me up and they give me a toy." Now think of how absurd that is to a child. What do you do when somebody is trying to rape somebody? You pick them up and give them a toy. Clearly what he was looking for was a model for what he was supposed to do. Mommy's situation was a domestic violence situation; a boyfriend was regularly physically assaulting her and raping her in front of this child. Everybody was assuming that he must have been abused based on his behavior. Emotionally, he

**Acting
Out**

was abused; but he wasn't sexually abused. People like to focus on false allegations of sexual abuse: it's much more common to have false recantation than it is to have a false allegation.

CI: In a therapeutic setting, is it ever possible or advisable to confront a victim and an abuser?

COLAO: To work with them together?

CI: Yes.

Joint Therapy of Victim and Abuser

COLAO: It's therapeutic if you've got the abuser willing to take responsibility for his or her behavior, willing to apologize to the child. Then it's very therapeutic as part of the treatment. The only other situation where it could be therapeutic is in a supervised visitation situation where it is therapeutic for the child to disempower the offender. From a child's perspective someone who abuses him and gets him to maintain the secret is an all-powerful monster that the child has to be frightened of the rest of his life. If you can have a carefully supervised situation where you can reassure the child, "Here, they are not going to be allowed to hurt you again; they are not going to be allowed to do or say anything that scares or upsets you, but you're gonna be able to see them and spend some time with them," that can really disempower the abuser to the child and it can also give the child confidence. Especially when you're dealing with incest situations, the child doesn't love or hate the abusive parent; he loves *and* hates the abusive parent. The child has a tremendous amount of ambivalence. As far as the child is concerned, there are good things about that parent. So providing a situation where the child can have permission for good feelings and not have to suffer abuse as a trade-off can be very therapeutic for the child, whether or not the offender enters into treatment.

CI: Is therapy typically a component in the child protective services response to abuse or neglect?

Therapy and Child Protective Services

COLAO: It's supposed to be, but from my experience, very often a judge will order treatment for a child and you will find out six months or a year later from maybe the fourth caseworker who's now on petition that, "Oh well, you know, he was on a waiting list at one place, and then the other place was too far for the foster mother to bring him, and no, we still haven't found therapy yet."

CI: What recourse does a citizen have who witnesses or is aware of abuse that is inadequately dealt with by the authorities?

COLAO: My usual response to that is first and foremost to create a paper trail. When you call a report in to protective services, get the name of the person who takes the call. When you are contacted as part of the follow-up, get the name of that person. Keep a record of everybody who has contacted you in relation to the case, and then write and say, "On January 10th, I called in that Johnny Doe was physically beaten by his father in front of our building. On January 12th, Mary Jane Smith called me to ask for details. I described the bruise I saw on the child's face at that point. On January 14th, Mary Jane Smith came to visit the child, and noted that there was a bruise on the child's face. The child stated that he fell down; the child's father was present during the interview." Create documentation of what went wrong. If you don't know all of that information, and sometimes you won't, write in the information that you do know. So you know you spoke with Mary Jane Smith, but you don't know what happened since. You do know that the child has remained in the home and has been abused again.

Dealing with Inadequate Response to Report

CI: Then what do you do with your documentation?

COLAO: I'd call it in again. I advise people to contact their local legislators, your congressional representative. Contact whoever professes to be concerned about children and give them documentation as to what's going on with this case. Show them what has gone wrong. My experience is that the more fuss created about a given case, the more likely it is to be resolved in the child's best interest. I tell this to social workers and caseworkers all the time. I have a friend who works in a battered-women's shelter. She had a situation where a woman who was regularly battered was going back to the home. She would stay in a shelter for a couple of months or sometimes a couple of weeks and then go back. She had children, and each time the social workers saw these children, they had been abused: sometimes teeth were knocked out; sometimes they had bruises. She called in reports several times. Then a child was killed at the home, and the death had been ruled an accident. The child had supposedly fallen out of the window—certainly that was a case of neglect, at least. The mother came back to the shelter and soon decided she was going to try to reconcile again. So my friend called another report in. She said, "I really fear for these other two children and this woman." The response was "Oh, well that case has been closed. It was ruled an accident." She said, "Fine, may I have your name and your supervisor's name, because after the next child is killed, when I make the call to

Persistence in Reporting

the *New York Times* and the *New York Daily News,* I want to be sure I report your names correctly." When you have to, use the media.

CI: On the other hand I should think the frustrations of working as a caseworker in a child protective services agency are such that those people deserve therapy of their own.

**Case-
workers'
Frustration**

COLAO: Absolutely, and that's why there is such high turnover, and that's why the good ones can't last a lot of times. They can't bear what's going on, unless they really are able to carve a niche for themselves. Social workers have said to me, "Well I've finally gotten to the point to where I say, 'It's not my kid.' " That concerns me. As far as I'm concerned somebody saying that shouldn't be in the field.

CI: In your book you say that a national hotline for child abuse is your primary wish for change in the field. That was several years ago. Do you have any additional wishes?

**Needed
Changes**

COLAO: Certainly you need community-based programs that are going to accurately follow up reports with a multidiscipli- nary approach—so that you don't have cases such as John Doe is an alcoholic who periodically beats up his wife, and once in a while smacks his kids, and it goes to the hotline and they say,"Yeah, but the kids aren't dead." That is what really hap- pens, you know. I call in cases sometimes and they say, "Why are *you* calling it in?" I'll say because I'm worried about this child's welfare. They tell me they visited this kid three months ago and he was ok; he didn't have any bruises on him. I'm concerned about a six-year-old, for example, being left in the care of a drunk who periodically loses control. I would like to see a community program that could be assigned to monitor such situ- ations and follow up on what's happening with that kid. Some- times when I call in those cases they say, "Oh, watch it for a few weeks, and then call us back if you're still concerned about the kid." Well, I wouldn't have called in the first place if I weren't concerned about the kid. We need interdisciplinary community- based programs so that there is a system for people to communi- cate with each other, especially in urban areas. In a single case, one person might have contact through his work at a hospital or at a community center; somebody else might have contact in the schools; somebody else might have contact at the mother's pro- gram; somebody else might have contact at the program the father's been in. But these people never talk to each other.

CI: I assume you're talking about a privately funded group.

COLAO: I think it could be either public or private, I'm just **Team** talking about interdisciplinary teams working in these situa- **Treatment** tions so that everybody gets to share information with every- body else involved. I think there needs to be a child-advocacy component where somebody has the job of really looking out for the child. Now the kind of care the child gets depends on the bias of the agency.

CI: Outside of court? Or do you mean ad litem programs?

COLAO: I'm talking about both. But yes, certainly outside of **Agency** court someone is needed to ask is this the best form of treatment **Bias** for this child, and not is this the best for the family. Sometimes what people consider to be the best form of treatment for the family is really quite neglectful to the child. Kids say to me, "Oh yeah, family therapy is where your mom and dad tell everybody how bad you are, where the counselor tells you to try to be better." That is the child's experience of it. I have one little boy who says, "Oh yeah. When we used to go to the counselor, that was three against one." So we need somebody who's really looking at the situation from the child's perspective, because it's very hard—almost impossible—to be the therapist for child and parents. Often a team approach is required.

CI: How about prevention?

COLAO: More prevention work needs to be done that's accurate **Prevention** for children.

CI: How do you do that?

COLAO: I think schools are certainly one place.

CI: Education, you mean?

COLAO: Education, absolutely. Community education as well as the direct work with the children. I think there need to be more educational materials that speak directly to children.

CI: Like your own S.A.F.E. Kids materials?

COLAO: Yes. That's just one example of educational aids that **Children's** really reflect what happens to children. Yesterday I did a pro- **Input on** gram with young teenagers and preadolescents, eleven through **Prevention** fourteen years old, where we were talking about personal **Programs** safety, alcohol, and drugs. I said to them, "what do you know about personal safety, alcohol and drugs?" Various kids raised their hands. I said, "what do your parents tell you?" "Well, your parents tell you just say no." "What do think of that?" "It doesn't work." "Ok, let's talk about why it doesn't work."

"It doesn't work because when you're at a party with your friends, and you really want to be friends with those people, and you don't want to be called a nerd, you don't just say no. It doesn't work because your dad gets drunk all the time anyway, and your mom lets him drive." The process has to involve children's input on any curriculum that's developed to deal with their safety or their well-being. That is not being done. Very few programs involve children in the development of the curriculum or in the development of information that's being used to teach. Just Say No is a great concept, but pretty useless. It's like "Don't talk to strangers." That really doesn't prepare you for daddy.

The S.A.F.E. Kit™ for kids includes the 48-page activity book, *Be a S.A.F.E Kid!*, a 30-minute audiocassette, an emergency contact ID tag, sticker, and the "I'm a Safe Kid" poster. S.A.F.E. kits may be ordered singly or in bulk. The price for unassembled kits is: 1-99, $5 each plus $1 per kit for postage and handling; 100-499, $3.25 each plus 75¢ per kit for postage and handling; 500-999, $2 each plus 75¢ per kit for postage and handling; 1000 or more, $1.25 each plus 25¢ per kit for postage and handling. For assembly add 25¢ per kit. To order, send a check or money order for the correct amount to SAFEKIT QUICKSEND, 7 Nowell Farme Road, Carlisle, MA 01741 (508) 371-0518.

5

Child Protective Agencies: How They Operate

Child protective services is a generic name given to the state agencies that usually operate under the auspices of the department of social services to provide services to maltreated children and their families. CPS agencies in the United States can be traced to the nineteenth century, but their present identity was formed by the wave of child-protection legislation of the past twenty-five years that dramatically and precipitously increased their duties. State CPS agencies received and were required to act upon an estimated 669,000 reports of child maltreatment in 1976; in 1986, CPS agencies handled an estimated 2,086,000 reports.

The requirements of money, people, facilities, and administration to accommodate such a dramatic increase in workload posed a major organizational challenge, which has been met with uneven success throughout the country. Nonetheless, CPS is, in most communities, an established and usually growing bureaucracy. An important effect of child maltreatment legislation has been the institution of basic CPS programs from state to state and the imposition of standards of operation from which the individual services offered in each state spring. The character of state CPS programs varies widely, but their purpose is more or less uniform.

With regard to particulars, each state processes maltreatment reports differently, either because the procedures are different, the facilities are different, or the state laws are different; nonetheless, the routine is similar enough so that it is possible to generalize about how maltreatment reports are handled by CPS. Each state is required to designate an agency—normally a division of the department of social services—that must maintain and publicize a phone number to receive reports of maltreatment committed by a caretaker. CPS must react within a set amount of time, usually forty-eight hours, to each case reported. As a result of federal legislation, each state requires certain professionals, called mandated reporters, to report all cases or suspected cases of child maltreatment. According to *Highlights of Official Child Neglect and Abuse Reporting 1986* 54 percent of all reports come from such professionals. Of nonprofessional reporters, most are friends, neighbors, and relatives of the victim or abuser; only 2 percent of reports come from victims or abusers themselves. When a case is reported, a decision is made, based on legal guidelines, how fully to investigate. If a child seems to be in imminent danger, he or she can normally be removed immediately from the home and taken into CPS custody until a determination is made about the safety of the child's home environment. If it appears that criminal laws have been violated, law enforcement may be notified and the district attorney may be asked to investigate the advisability of criminal action. (Court action of any description is initiated in only about one-fourth of reported cases. Only a small percentage of these actions is filed in criminal court. Normally child maltreatment is heard primarily in family court or its equivalent. See pages 75-78.)

Sub-stantiation
In the majority of cases, CPS investigates over a prescribed period, normally of several weeks for a full investigation, before making a determination of substantiation. By that time, many cases are withdrawn from CPS consideration for one reason or another; for example, the child or the abuser being investigated may move to another jurisdiction; the status of the child may change as a grandmother or some other family member takes voluntary custody; or the caseworker, in consultation with the family, determines that the abuse is not — relative to other more demanding cases—seriously threatening and agrees to file it away. Cases that remain active at the end of the investigation period are designated substantiated or unsubstantiated at the discretion of the CPS caseworker. If cases are substantiated, action is required by CPS to safeguard the child. If cases are unsubstantiated, the investigation is dropped and the family may be referred to a prevention program.

Caseworkers' Dilemma
However carefully laws are drawn and however efficiently programs are organized, their effectiveness is finally dependent on the abilities, the judgment, the perceptiveness, and the energy of the CPS caseworker. Inevitably caseloads are unreasonably heavy and the emotional toll is wearing.

State child-protective agencies have developed step-by-step procedure manuals instructing caseworkers and supervisors about their responsibilities in various situations. The *Policy and Procedure Manual of the South Carolina Department of Social Services* is a model.

South Carolina warns child protective services staff that they must often weigh the rights of parents against the rights of children. When they conflict, the rights of the children are given priority (some states reverse the priority), even if it means removing the child from his home. In South Carolina, those rights are stipulated this way:

The rights of children: **The Rights of Children**

1) Full support for the meeting of basic needs.

2) Protection.

3) Diagnosis and treatment of any medical condition.

4) An education provided by state law.

5) A stable and nurturing environment.

6) Inheritance from one's parents.

7) Being in the physical custody of one's parents when it is in one's best interests.

8) Protection of those rights guaranteed by the Constitution.

The rights of parents: **The Rights of Parents**

The right of custody given the parent includes the right of possession and the right to discipline the child. It carries with it responsibilities that must be assumed by the parent. These are to support, supervise, and provide for the general welfare of the child.

The right of guardianship is the right the parents retain during   **The Rights of Guardians**
the child's minority, and it continues even if the right of custody
is removed by the court.

Guardianship entails the right to:

1) Consent to all major medical services.

2) Permit the marriage of a child below the age of consent.

3) Permit a minor child to enter the military.

4) Consent to the adoption of a child unless the court has terminated parental rights.

5) Provide proper legal notice about any delinquent acts

alleged to be committed by one's child.

6) Inherit from one's children.

7) Visit with one's child or children, only to be terminated by the court.

Perspective: Attacking the Problem

Andrew Vachss

Andrew Vachss has served as a field investigator for the U.S. Public Health Service; a casework supervisor for the New York City Department of Social Services; special investigator in Biafra, during the Nigerian civil war, for the Save the Children Federation and the Community Development Foundation; deputy director of the Medfield-Norfolk Prison Project; director of the Intensive Treatment Unit, a maximum security prison for juveniles and youths, under the auspices of the Massachusetts Department of Youth Services; planner and analyst in the Yonkers, New York, Crime Control Coordinator's Office; and, since 1976, an attorney limiting himself to matters concerning children.

CI: How much credence do you place in the various surveys about the prevalence of child abuse and neglect?

VACHSS: I don't place much. The media, which have been, despite my criticism, the only real force for social change in the area of child maltreatment, have increased awareness. That has without question increased case reporting. But there's no hard evidence to indicate that a 300% increase in reporting means a 300% increase in cases. I am not myself convinced, except for certain technological changes, that there's any more child abuse going on today than there was twenty years ago.

Accuracy of Statistics

CI: The latest National Incidence Study supports that conclusion.

VACHSS: The problem with any of these surveys is that it's very easy to play with them. But basically the surveys represent a swinging pendulum. There was a time when any kid who complained of incest was judged to be nuts and treated as somebody with psychotic fantasy. Now people are saying that one out of every four children in this country will have been sexually abused by the age of eighteen. I find that equally ludicrous from my ground-zero point of view.

CI: How do you combine your law practice with your interest in the welfare of children?

Vachss's Law Practice

VACHSS: My law practice is exclusively limited to the representation of children and youth. That encompasses everything from defending a child accused of a crime to representing a child who is the victim of one, and everything in between, including civil litigation, adoptions, representing children who are the battleground in a divorce—there's no limit to it.

CI: How do you define juvenile?

Definition of Juvenile

VACHSS: I define juvenile as anyone younger than an adult.

CI: Is there an age limit? Suppose a twenty-five-year-old comes to you with a problem.

VACHSS: If a twenty-five-year-old comes to me—and this has happened—and says, "I was sexually abused by my father when I was eleven, and I wasn't able to discuss it or do anything about it because I was in kind of a psychiatric coma; but I've been in therapy for three or four years, and now I want to do something about it," I wouldn't exclude her as a client.

CI: But the action that is taking you to court has to have occurred when the child was under eighteen, say?

VACHSS: Yes, generally.

CI: How many lawyers are engaged in the practice of juvenile defense?

Scarcity of Lawyers in Juvenile Justice

VACHSS: I just got a copy of *Who's Who in American Law, 1990.* In order to find a place for me—my category is "Children and Youth"—they simply put me under "Other." I looked through everybody else in "Other," and there are some fairly exotic specialties, but none listed as "Children and Youth." There are lawyers who do exclusively juvenile defense, but they tend to be people who work for a public defender's office, assigned to juvenile defense.

CI: Is that because kids don't normally have enough money to hire attorneys?

VACHSS: That's part of it, and they are also extremely difficult clients. But I think the main reason is that it's not a lucrative practice. Also it is not even mentioned in law school, much less taught.

CI: How are you brought together with a child who needs your help?

VACHSS: One way is that parents or guardians are accused of abusing their child. The law doesn't permit them to hire a lawyer for the child for obvious reasons—they'd be in conflict. On the other hand, the government entity which is prosecuting them for child abuse really represents the government agency, not the child. The child has independent interests, so the law provides for independent counsel. That counsel is appointed like a rotating wheel. You have to qualify to be on the wheel, and then when your number comes up, you're assigned to a specific case.

How Juveniles Get Legal Help

CI: So you're sort of like a public defender?

VACHSS: Sort of, except that you're private. You're not required to take any case, and you're not paid a salary. Indeed, all this talk about pro bono is pretty funny, since the wages that the government pays you to do this work are something like an eighth of what the average lawyer gets. But the way I've just described isn't the only way I get to represent kids. I've been hired directly by kids; now we're talking about teenagers. I've been hired by parents or caretakers to represent a child against a third party, for example, when a child is abused in a day-care center or by a youth group leader. I'm also referred cases by everybody from doctors to cops to nurses to social workers.

Independent Counsel for Justice

CI: Do child abuse cases constitute the majority of your work?

VACHSS: Yes, in one way or another they do, especially since in a number of so-called juvenile delinquency cases I've handled there's proved to be significant child abuse in the children's background. I don't represent a kid who's been in a car accident.

CI: It would seem that your involvement with child abuse as a children's advocate would be limited to the most severe cases. Of the six catogories of maltreatment, which command your attention most frequently?

VACHSS: It's very hard for me to answer that simply, because I find the types comingling. I never find discrete, statutorily-perfect child abuse. Prototypically, a child is an incest victim of her father, with the knowledge and complicity but not direct participation of the mother. The child's younger brother sees all this going on and is raised in this sexually perverted, highly aggressive household and is emotionally abused by that. So you have abuse, neglect, and emotional neglect all in the same pot. I've represented children in circumstances in which they have literally been driven to suicide attempts and not a hand was placed on them; they were never touched in any way. People

Types of Cases

always ask me what's the worst type of child abuse. It is obvious from the question that they are looking at the problem not from the viewpoint of the victim, but from that of the observer. Worst is whatever's happening to the child.

CI: *Worst* is a subjective word.

VACHSS: Absolutely. And one person may think, depending on his particular personal take, that a priest molesting a child is the worst type of abuse, because it is the abuse of a religious trust. Another might say a father doing it, because that's the abuse of a parental trust. Some might say physical torture is worse than sexual abuse that doesn't involve violence. Others might say killing a child is the worst. I don't think it matters from a child's perspective.

CI: It would seem that emotional neglect might be just as traumatic for a kid as physical abuse.

Emotional Neglect

VACHSS: I can give you proof: the proof is that physical injury heals. You don't need to go further than that. When you see somebody still in post-traumatic stress disorder ten or fifteen years after the event, or you see somebody acting out grotesquely, insanely, or criminally as a result of what was done to him as a child, it's not because he can still see the burn marks. It's because the emotional baggage is stronger than any other. The other way you can prove that point is this: sexually molested children who are molested by caretakers have far more difficult recovery periods than those molested by strangers. A kid who's molested in his own house has to carry the burden of guilt for that molestation as well as the pain. If you're molested by strangers, you look to family members to comfort you. If those same comforters are actually the abusers, you exacerbate the trauma.

CI: Your work must depend heavily on investigation.

Investigation and Therapy in Child Abuse Cases

VACHSS: Almost exclusively. Without quality investigation, you can't prove your case, and I either do it or direct it. I have personally investigated cases and still do, especially the interrogation that is part of investigation. I have a team of people who are necessary, because it's not simply like a private eye looking for clues. You also need very skilled therapists. Sometimes you need a person who's trained in clinical hypnosis; sometimes you need a doctor who can use a regression form of hypnosis aided by something like sodium amytal. Sometimes you need people who can go places where other people don't want to go, and there you'd more likely use a private investigator. It's a combination of different kinds of people that you need for these cases.

CI: It sounds very expensive.

VACHSS: It probably would be, but over the years I've put together a crew of people. I get calls from people I don't know—people who saw me on television or read about me in a book—who get in touch to say that they're good at some part of this process, and if I ever need help, to give them a call.

Attorneys' Support

CI: So if they aren't strictly volunteers, they are people willing to devote themselves to the work for reasons other than remuneration?

VACHSS: Yes. But that doesn't mean it's not expensive. We are serving a client, so if I undertake a case—let's say a civil lawsuit—it's my requirement that the child be in therapy. I won't represent a child who isn't, because we don't want to make our own damages. Say a child is raped in a day-care center. If you don't give the kid therapy, by the time the case comes to trial you have a wonderful little basket case to put on the stand. If you do provide therapy, the kid is far more oriented and focused, and appears to be less damaged.

CI: We read in the paper about psychologists and social workers who are themselves able to manipulate children in these cases. How do you respond to that?

VACHSS: Anyone can manipulate anybody if the power relationships are appropriate. I don't deny that a psychologist can manipulate a child, nor would anybody deny that a parent or a significant caretaker can manipulate a child. You hear the point about manipulation raised most often in matrimonial litigation. Typically, the mother says that the father abused the child, and the father claims the mother brainwashed the child.

Validity of Juvenile Testimony in Court

CI: As in the highly publicized recent case of Dr. Elizabeth Morgan, who just got out of jail after serving a term for not allowing her daughter to see the father as stipulated by a court order?

VACHSS: That's a classic example. Of course, what that child has to say is of almost no value now. The child has been seen by too many people over too long a period of time under too much pressure. You'd have to sort the truth out of it all by an independent investigation; it wouldn't come out of the child's mouth

Morgan Case

anymore. Children are not different from adults. They can lock into a reward-punishment syndrome and respond in a way that they think is going to be best for them. But there are things you can do about this, and I'll give you one simple example. Let's say a kid has been coached by Mommy. He says to me, "Daddy did this; Daddy did that"—the whole litany. Then you ask the questions out of sequence and see if you get the same result. Assuming that you do, now you've got a whole list of things that the child says were done to him. Now you ask a very simple jackpot question: How did it *feel?* It's very hard to program somebody about feelings. It's fairly easy to do it around recollections, but feelings are a whole different story. The other thing that I want to stress is that I use independent verifiers. If I have a report of abuse, I will send the kid to one person for verification and maybe another person entirely for treatment. I don't rely strictly on anybody's statement. Corroboration is the name of the game. Also, I don't put psychologists in a position to benefit from manipulation. When we hire therapists for children, they're paid. That's it. They don't get a bonus if we're successful in a lawsuit.

CI: In news reports of child abuse cases, it often seems an act of cruelty to put a child through the system of examination and cross-examination required to get a conviction. How do you feel about this?

Victims' Testimony

VACHSS: I profoundly disagree. I think the media have done a horrible disservice to all of us in describing this process, whether out of concern or out of laziness I don't know. Is it cruelty to have a three-year-old child swim? No. But it could be if the child didn't know how to swim. Court testimony is exactly the same thing. The truth is that, in an overwhelming majority of my cases in which I've had kids testify, it was an empowering experience rather than traumatizing. The effect has to do with preparing the child for what's going to happen and working therapeutically with the child around his expectations. Certainly if you simply put a child in a chair and started screaming at him, it would be traumatic; it would be for anybody. But the media view of what it's like isn't what it needs to be like. I also think it's in the interest of pedophiles and all child abusers to keep spreading this negative message through the media. That encourages good-spirited, good-hearted people not to pursue cases.

CI: I assume that, in the interest of the accused's rights, there are no restraints at all on questioning children in court, except for the normal judicial rules on cross-examination; so an attorney can be as ruthless as the law permits.

VACHSS: Yes. But whether it's effective or not can depend on who's on the jury. Jurors are human beings, and some of them just don't like to see children abused. The only thing that's really different in these trials, despite all the rhetoric, is that to some extent, in some jurisdictions, you can physically shield the child from having to eyeball the perpetrator, whether this means testifying on closed-circuit television, or testifying behind a screen, or simply having the furniture arranged in such a way that there doesn't have to be direct eye-to-eye contact. And a child has his or her own defenses too. If you scream at a child enough, the child just starts to cry or melts down. That doesn't necessarily mean that he's lying, and most people understand that. Sure, it can be a horrible experience for kids. It's not fun for anybody to testify in court. But you've got to remember that if a child was abused, essentially what was abused was a power relationship. It's a horrible feeling of helplessness to be at the mercy of an abuser. In court, despite all the screaming and yelling, nobody's going to physically or sexually abuse a child. And very often we're confronted with this reality: if you do the warm, caring thing of not having the child testify, it could mean that he goes back and lives with the abuser.

Cross-examination of Victims

CI: Are court-appointed advocates, such as guardians ad litem, useful in protecting a child's rights and guarding against what might be called judicial child abuse?

VACHSS: I want to be very, very clear about this. Are they useful? The answer is, they can be. Are they ever a substitute for actual representation by lawyers? No. Underline no. Repeat, NO. I think that concept represents one of the most pernicious trends in child protective work in this country today. There are states—and Florida is an excellent example—where a child who is the victim of abuse will not be represented by a lawyer but will be represented by a court-appointed special advocate. These people are not lawyers. Because they're not lawyers, they can't represent a child in terms of the totality of that child's needs. They can't file a motion. They can't argue before a court with any kind of force. I'll give you some concrete examples. If a child tells a secret to a court-appointed special advocate there is no attorney-client privilege. That child is not guaranteed the confidentiality that he would have in speaking to an attorney. We have a standard in American justice called effective assistance of counsel. Under that standard, if you're accused of a crime and your lawyer is incompetent, your case

Court Appointed Advocates

could be reversed, because you're entitled to minimal effectiveness. No non-lawyer can meet that standard. The whole Court Appointed Special Advocate concept gets its power from the idea that it's cheap; it's cost-effective. That's utter nonsense. You look at a state like Florida that could provide a stream of attorneys for a Ted Bundy and can't provide one attorney for an abused child. I think there's such a moral difficulty with that, that it's unresolvable.

CI: On the other hand, in the typical case, can an attorney who has a busy workload be expected to provide the kinds of out-of-court support that a child in difficulty might need?

Guardian Ad Litem as Substitute for Attorney

VACHSS: I don't know what "out-of-court support" means. I know that a lawyer is supposed to do his job, and if that job involves out-of-court support services, those services are supposed to be provided. If the attorney doesn't have the personal resources, the attorney makes application to the court for such resources. I think the idea of having a lay person involved who's going to be sort of a friend to the kid and watch out for the kid and visit the kid and all that stuff is really valuable. However, I don't think that person can ever be a substitute for an attorney. That's the bone of contention here.

CI: But does the guardian ad litem program suggest that the guardian is an attorney-substitute?

VACHSS: Absolutely. The ad litem program takes the position, what do you need lawyers for? Lawyers for kids are no good anyway. They're lazy, they're overworked, they're incompetent—blah, blah, blah. You scratch those people and they will bleed the belief that lawyers really don't belong in child abuse court.

CI: Is it your feeling that the ad litem program ought not to be done away with but rather altered so that the guardian works under the supervision of the attorney who's directing the case?

Ad Litem Support

VACHSS: I don't believe that they have to be under anybody's supervision. They can be independent all they want. They can be the strongest advocates for the kid they want. In fact I'd like to see them here saying the lawyer's not doing his job. I don't want them subservient to anybody. I just don't want them as a substitute for counsel. Here's the ridiculousness of it: If I'm a kid twelve years old in a state that has this wonderful program instead of attorneys for kids and I'm an abused kid and I want an attorney, you know what I have to do? Commit a crime. Then the law guarantees I have an attorney. The reasoning of the law is this: Children in a juvenile court who are accused of delinquency are entitled to an attorney because they risk serious consequences, such as being incarcerated. Since when is being returned to abusers or molesters not a serious consequence? I think if children could vote, this guardian ad litem as substitution for lawyers would last about thirty seconds. You could go ask somebody who's charged with an SEC violation if he wants a warm, caring volunteer or a lawyer who's an expert in the field. Nobody's asked the kids yet. If they're sincere, then their program ought to be able to stand on its merits. Where it stands today is that it's cheap. It doesn't cost anything.

CI: A change of subject. How widespread is child pornography?

VACHSS: To understand that question, I have to determine if you understand the difference between width and depth. When people ask that question, they want the usual nonsensical statistics. That doesn't help. Let me explain why. Crime chases dollars. Those people in a position to produce pornography have determined, and rightly so, that every pedophile is an inexhaustible well, so that one pedophile would, if he could, possess all the kiddie pornography in the world. You find that the well is being filled, and that product is created to fill it. How many porn buyers are there? Nobody could know, but those that do exist are consumers with a voracity that you can't imagine. Therefore, when you ask how widespread it is, are you talking about the amount produced, the amount consumed, the width or the depth? Those are the things you have to look at.

Child Pornography

CI: Do you see a direct link between pornography and child sexual abuse?

VACHSS: Yes. But what kind of pornography are you talking about? It has to be defined.

CI: Do you want to define it?

VACHSS: My definition is that kiddie pornography is the photograph of a crime, and therefore per se illegal in my view; it should be prosecuted as such. What I mean by pornography is the graphic depiction of sexual activity. Pornography is certainly connected to sexual abuse when it's used by predators to desensitize victims. If a predator has a ten-year-old boy in the house and shows him photographs of ten-year-old boys engaged in sexual activity, and the kid sees enough of it, his impression—especially if he sees it on videotape—is that this is happening, this is OK, and his thresholds are reduced. That's one

Definition of Child Pornography

distinct way pornography and child abuse are connected. Another way they're connected is through the product. Under my definition the producers have criminally abused children sexually to produce that pornography. I do not agree that anybody who reads *Playboy* magazine is a deviant.

CI: Is it correct to assume that there are a few centers where people are producing magazines, videotapes, photos?

VACHSS: That's right and wrong. There are a few centers where magazines are being produced, but there are countless places in which porn is generated. Child pornography is pretty much a cottage industry now. Any deviant with a Polaroid camera or a hand-held camcorder can make his own stuff. It's not made commercially in the sense that they'd make five hundred copies of a Polaroid shot, but it certainly is trafficked in.

CI: Do you have a means of tracking the activity of chronic child abusers?

Tracking Pedophiles

VACHSS: I keep a computer database of two kinds of information. One is highly specific information involving cases I have personally worked, because I'm constantly looking for correlations and for things to kick in from the past. It's been enormously helpful in literally solving cases. But also in there is a huge amount of information that I've obtained outside my personal caseloads. Most of that comes in over the transom. People hear about what I do and send me stuff. Some of it relates to child pornography. I also have received audiotapes, pictures, letters that purport to be from and about rather famous people, alleging that these people are predatory pedophiles. Clearly the people sending such material are sending it for a reason. I don't fancy myself the police force, but every piece of information we get is checked, and the idea is to keep in the computer only information that we're absolutely satisfied is true. I'm not privy to police records, and the police don't tell me whom they've just arrested.

CI: Do the police track the activity of pedophiles?

Registering Pedophiles

VACHSS: I don't know. But I do know that—except, I believe, in California—convicted offenders are not even required to register with the local police. That means that in most jurisdictions a guy who has been involved in child pornography and has a record of abusing children can get a job as a schoolteacher or working in a nursery or day-care center. It happens in New

York all the time.

CI: Are you an advocate of a federal law to require such registration?

VACHSS: Yes, a federal law to require it, on a central computer database. But that's not enough. What is critically needed is a law requiring that any place employing people to work with kids must check with that registry, and that if they fail to do so, the employers are strictly liable for whatever happens. That would give employers the strongest financial incentive to use the registry.

CI: Is there any federal attempt to track the activities of child abusers? I assume that would fall within the auspices of the FBI.

VACHSS: There is an FBI pedophile task force, though I'm not sure what it does. I don't know of any effort actually to track the movements of such people.

CI: You stated that the juvenile offenders you defend are often child abuse victims. Would you elaborate on that?

VACHSS: Basically there are only two ways to account for criminality: criminals are born, and criminals are made. There's obviously some dispute on that, but I don't think any rational person in 1990 disputes anymore that there are specific ways in which the twig can be bent so that you can get a very evil tree. I have never represented a predatory, life-style-violent kid who did not have significant child abuse in his background. That doesn't mean that every kid who goes joyriding or throws a brick through a window— or even every kid who shoots somebody—was a child abuse victim. But it certainly means to me that when you have a depraved kind of crime such as rape, sodomy, or stabbing a little kid, you're going to see a reason for it. And consistently what emerges is that we have an abused child now acting out. It's important for me to say at this point that explanation is not justification. I'm not saying that anybody has a get-out-of-jail-free card because he's an abused child. What I'm saying is that this knowledge we have could help us interdict the worst kind of criminality before it flowers.

Offenders as Victims

CI: What kind of interdiction would you suggest?

VACHSS: I suggest, very bluntly, that the only genuine crime prevention program in America, without question, is child protective services, which provide people to investigate and proceed against child abusers.

The Need for Better Child Protective Services

CI: Is there a model program?

VACHSS: There may be some minor-league model program somewhere, but what I am talking about is government action. It's strictly a government function.

CI: You are suggesting an ambitious and complicated network of psychologists, social workers, investigators?

VACHSS: Absolutely, with professionals at the legal end as well, to handle these cases in court. Such a program should be well funded and have highly recruited, highly trained personnel. It should be seen as an opportunity to change the course of America's future. Instead, we have quite the opposite situation: child protection programs are basically the garbage can of social services.

CI: What you're talking about now is political action, because it would take political force to set up such a system. Are there any politicians, particularly on a national level, who've expressed an interest in the problem?

Political Response to Child Abuse

VACHSS: No, not to me. There are plenty of organizations that live on grants and are constantly giving politicians awards. But I don't see the evidence of any such effort. We have a war on drugs that is universally described as ludicrous and a failure, and yet nobody begrudges multibillion-dollar injections into it. Child protection services are the least trained, least paid, least respected professionals out there.

CI: You must see the effects of drugs every minute of your day, and the effect from generation to generation of drug users. Cocaine-addicted babies are news now, for example, and I know you've had cases involving addicted mothers. Recently you had a case in which you got custody of the fetus of a drug-addicted mother.

Drugs and Abuse

VACHSS: Yes. That case is just over, by the way; the child has been freed for adoption. You must understand, though, that, unlike the way it was reported, that case wasn't about cocaine addiction. The fact that the child was born with a positive toxology for cocaine had nothing whatever to do with it; it was purely circumstance. We had a mother who was a serial child-abuse offender, and this was unequivocally not related to her own drug abuse. In fact, she is the example I use all the time when people like Bennett say, "Well, if we legalize drugs, we're going to have kids born addicted," and "Drugs are causing child abuse." This is a woman who abused children before crack existed, and, because of her life-style and personality, got involved with drugs and continued to do what she had always done: to wit, abuse children.

CI: Nonsexual physical abuse?

VACHSS: Yes. These kids were beaten badly enough to require significant medical attention. When this woman became pregnant, it was clear to me that we were facing the situation of having a child born into an environment which had produced several other abused children. As a preemptive strike, I sought a court order saying that, upon the child's birth, he would be in imminent danger of abuse and should be removed from her custody.

Fetal Custody

CI: What does "preemptive strike" mean?

VACHSS: By "preemptive strike" I simply mean that I wasn't waiting for the baby to be born. It had nothing to do with fetal rights; it was saying that an event is going to take place, and when it does, we're going to have a child in danger. I want to have the court order in my hand before that time. The entire intent was to do what all the good-hearted liberals say they want to do and cannot do, which is to prevent child abuse. Everyone talks about prevention. Everyone loves prevention. It's cheap; it's cost-effective to talk about it. My position is that you can't prevent child abuse. By and large child abuse isn't preventable. In this case it was.

CI: Are there types of child abusers?

VACHSS: There are three types— understand that these are general categories with some overlap. First, there are the inadequates, who simply don't know how to parent. A good example is a twelve-year-old girl with a baby of her own. Such people benefit immeasurably from so-called rehabilitative services. They really can be helped, and they deserve all our efforts. The second category is people who are crazy (and by that I mean card-carrying crazy), and the third is people who are evil. The distinct problem we have is that we merge one category into another and ignore the third. When someone sodomizes a baby, it's likely to be said that that person is "sick." That's wrong. When somebody does something outrageous to a child, we say the person is crazy, and that's often wrong. Social work doesn't recognize the concept of evil; it's not part of their "dynamic." There has to be a cold-blooded attempt to separate the categories and to respond accordingly on a pure triage model. That is, we must put every effort into what can be saved, but not waste precious resources in trying to save what cannot be.

Types of Abusers

CI: How do you feel about mandatory sterilization of parents, male and female, who are proven irresponsible?

Court-ordered VACHSS: I'm a hundred percent opposed to it, not because of
Sterilization the right of the parent, but because it reminds me too much of the Third Reich. I don't know where it would stop. We might be comfortable about making a decision about sterilization today about those people who are so over the line that we have to make that decision about them, but I don't know where that line would blur tomorrow. I don't want to be in a society that sterilizes humans against their will. The next thing you know, we'd start sterilizing defectives and inadequates. I don't know where it would stop.

CI: If somebody is interested in finding out more about child maltreatment not as a researcher but as an individual who is concerned about the problem and wants to help, where can he go?

What VACHSS: I can give you the names of specific places where
Concerned people can find out more about child abuse, but the second part,
Citizens help, is a complicated issue. It's one thing if you want the names
Can Do of places where people can go to use their own skills in working with kids. But if by "help" you mean changing the system, that's an entirely different answer. The organization that I'm happiest with is called the Children's Safety Project, and it's right here in Manhattan. Anyone willing to put in a relatively small amount of time in such a place would learn more than they ever wanted to know about every form of child abuse, and be able to be of service. They have used people there whose skills range from martial arts to working with clay to custodial care. This organization directly treats abused children. It doesn't do consciousness-raising, doesn't do informational brochures, doesn't hold conferences, doesn't give plaques, doesn't have dinners. It works directly with victims of abuse, every day, and it works with them not just therapeutically, but in an empowerment way. It prepares them for court; it prepares them to deal with the rest of their lives, not just the individual trauma.

CI: What can people do who are interested in influencing legislation?

Influencing VACHSS: There's only one way to do that, and that's by the
Legislation development of a single-issue, megalomaniacal group modeled on (I say this with all due respect) Mothers Against Drunk Driving. Or, if you want to go the other way, the antiabortion people, or the National Rifle Association. You need a group that

says to a politician, "I care nothing about your stand on El Salvador or the environment. I don't care about anything except this one issue. And my response to you is strictly dependent on your response to this issue. If you vote in favor of what I want, I will knock myself out to support you, I will raise funds; I will do everything I can to see that you're elected and stay elected. If, however, you oppose it, regardless of what you do on other issues I will work just as hard for your opponent."

CI: And there's no place to start except at the very beginning, if this is your interest?

VACHSS: Yes, I absolutely believe so.

CI: We hear more and more about criminal groups recruiting children to commit crimes that have high exposure and a high risk of being caught, so that if the kid is caught, he goes through the juvenile system and doesn't have to worry about the same kind of penalties an adult would risk. Is there any way to confront that problem?

VACHSS: Yes. Right now we have very flabby laws concerning exploitation of children. We have laws that say you're not supposed to rape children—although, of course, if you rape your own child, that's incest and it's considered family dysfunction. But leaving that aside, we seriously need laws that specifically say the utilization of children for criminal purposes is an independently actionable crime, and it should be a very serious major-felony one.

Criminals Recruiting Children

CI: Would that be on a national level or a local level?

VACHSS: I don't believe in local levels; that just encourages bad people to change jurisdictions. I don't believe in federal laws, because federal law enforcement isn't generally at the street level. What I believe in is uniform laws. Any lack of uniformity promotes injustice. I think there need to be irreducible minimums; in other words, if you do x to a child, the minimum you can look at is y response, whether you're in Alaska or Alabama.

Federal Response

CI: Is there somebody paying attention to this problem?

VACHSS: There may be. The government funds an enormous amount of stuff. I'm particularly fond of the example in which some crony of Ed Meese's was given about a million dollars to study whether *Playboy* and *Penthouse* were causing juvenile delinquency. We have something called the Office of Juvenile Justice and Delinquency Prevention. If you ask around among people in the field, they won't be able to tell you what this place

Paying Attention

does, except give grants. We don't have a Pentagon in this war that's being fought concerning children. We need a wartime mentality and a separate agency that is specifically going to protect children, and it should be constituted in the guise of crime prevention. It's very simple: If the American public bought the proposition that today's victim is tomorrow's predator, then out of self-interest, which is the great American motivator, we would see a change in the laws and in the enforcement of those laws as that enforcement affects kids. That's the bottom line. Those young human beings who are running around scaring us to death had a genesis. If we accept that that genesis was child abuse and neglect when they were much younger, we have a chance not just to do some good, but to do some good for ourselves.

6

Child Maltreatment and the Courts

Most reported cases of child maltreatment never go to court— they are handled by child protective services and judicial action is averted. When the court does become involved, it may be in four general ways, though a single case may involve proceedings in more than one court.

Introduction

1) In criminal proceedings, in which an alleged offender is charged with a crime and faces penalties exacted by the state— normally of imprisonment, community service, probation (with or without court-mandated psychiatric treatment of the offender), a fine. Child abuse and, in some states, certain forms of neglect are subject to criminal prosecution. In practice, however, criminal action is reserved for only the most extreme cases.

Criminal Court

2) In civil proceedings in which an adult, normally a caretaker, alleged to be guilty of maltreatment or to have acted or failed to act in such a way as to have caused maltreatment is sued for damages on the child's behalf. In such actions, the court is requested to order financial compensation to the child for damages he or she may have suffered. In some cases an additional financial award of punitive damages may also be ordered.

Civil Court

3) In matrimonial proceedings in which maltreatment becomes an issue in determining custody of the child.

Divorce Court

4) In family court (sometimes called juvenile court or dependency court) proceedings in which the court is asked to determine whether a child is maltreated and act in the best interests of the child to provide protection against abusive or neglectful behavior by a parent or other caretaker. Such cases vary greatly and cannot be categorized easily; it can be said, though, that the court typically decides whether to remove the child from the parents' custody, temporarily or permanently, or whether to order some protective measures for the child—such as counseling or training for the parents. Most cases of child maltreatment

Family Court

that come to court are heard by a family court judge.

**Parental
Custody**

According to the American Humane Association, in 1986 the parent was named as the perpetrator in 80.1% of the reports of child maltreatment. That statistic suggests the most sensitive issue regarding child abuse: Under what circumstances should a child be removed from the custody of his parents? This issue has been addressed by federal legislation regulating foster care and mandating that children who are removed from their homes be returned at the earliest opportunity without endangering the child.

**Revocation
of
Custody**

Child protective agencies typically have strictly defined guidelines for recommending court-ordered removal of a child from his parents' custody. These are the guidelines stipulated by the South Carolina Department of Social Services in its *Policies and Procedure Manual.*

**Imminent
Danger**

When imminent danger exists, a child may be removed by law enforcement, the family court judge, or medical personnel. If a law-enforcement officer removes the child, a court order must be obtained, within 72 hours in many states. Imminent danger refers to an emergency situation in which the welfare or life of the child is threatened and in which serious harm is likely to occur in the immediate future, such as:

1) Prostitution, coerced sexual intercourse, or coerced sexual exploitation.

2) Nonaccidental trauma, such as burns or lacerations intentionally inflicted by a parent, guardian, caretaker, sibling, or babysitter. A babysitter is defined as a person who provides care or supervision for children by agreement with the children's parents or caretaker, or other persons who are in control of the children.

3) Nutritional deprivation in circumstances involving a nonorganic failure to thrive. Deprivation to a child who is under the age of five or who is handicapped occurs when the child is malnourished and/or dehydrated and is in immediate jeopardy of loss of life or subject to permanent impairment unless treatment is provided in the ensuing few hours.

4) Abandonment.

5) A condition requiring emergency medical treatment. A condition which, if left untreated for a short period of time, will likely result in physical damage such as profuse or arterial

bleeding, major dislocation or fracture, unconsciousness, or evidence of ingestion of significant amounts of a poisonous substance.

6) Substantial emotional injury signifying imminent danger to the physical well being of the child. Such danger includes the inability or unwillingness of a parent or guardian to take precautionary measures regarding a child's threat of suicide. No other emergency situation involving mental injury may be a valid basis for removal without judicial authorization.

A child may also be removed immediately or under judicial authorization when:

Other Reasons to Revoke Custody

1) Parents refuse to obtain medical care for the child.

2) A child's physical/emotional damage is such that the child needs an extremely supportive environment in which to recuperate.

3) A child's sex, age, or condition renders him incapable of self-protection and for some reason constitutes a characteristic the parents find completely intolerable.

4) Evidence indicates that the parents are torturing the child or systematically resorting to physical force which bears no relation to reasonable discipline.

5) The physical environment of the home poses an immediate threat to the child. Evidence indicates that parental anger and discomfort with the investigation will be directed toward the child in the form of severe retaliation.

6) Evidence indicates that parents are out of touch with reality and they cannot provide for the child's basic needs.

7) Evidence indicates that the parents' physical condition poses a threat to the child.

8) The family has a history of hiding the child from outsiders.

9) There is a history of long-term sexual abuse or evidence suggests that the sexual abuse is escalating.

10) The family has a history of prior incidents or allegations of abuse or neglect.

11) The parents are completely unwilling to cooperate in an investigation or to maintain contact with any social agency, or may flee the jurisdiction.

12) Following the removal of the originally reported victim, there is no evidence that the removal reduced any stress or other influencing negative elements and there are other children who now may be at risk.

Perspective: Child Abuse in Criminal Court

James M. Peters

James M. Peters is a senior attorney with the National Center for Prosecution of Child Abuse, which is a subsection of the American Prosecutor's Research Institute, the training and technical assistance arm of the National District Attorneys Association. The National Center for Prosecution of Child Abuse was created in 1985 in response to a perception on the part of local prosecutors around the country that child abuse was an area in which prosecutors had not done an adequate job. It provides technical assistance, training, research, and help on trial strategy for prosecutors, police officers, social workers, psychologists, CPS caseworkers, and others involved in child abuse cases. Besides Mr. Peters, the National Center for Prosecution for Child Abuse staff also includes its director, Patricia Toth, a former director of the child abuse unit in Snohomish County in Everett, Washington; and senior attorney Jill Hiatt, who was previously a director of the child abuse unit in the Alameda County District Attorney's office in Oakland, California. Other professional staff include attorneys Eva Klain and Joy Repella and communications director Janet Dinsmore.

CI: In a typical local district attorney's office, would there be a prosecutor who specializes in child abuse?

PETERS: There is no typical office. It varies from location to location and depends a lot on the size of the office. There are some rural counties which may have only a part-time prosecutor and a couple of part-time deputies. In that case, certainly they do not have a specialist. On the other hand, many metropolitan offices and even smaller offices in suburbs have realized the need for specialization. Specialization among prosecutors is something that we advocate here at the National Center, because child abuse cases are unique, and we don't learn how to deal with them in law school.

Typical Prosecutor

CI: Do you have any sense of how many specialist prosecutors and defense attorneys there are in the area of child abuse?

**Abuse
Specialists**

PETERS: We have identified over eight hundred specialist prosecutors, but that information is nearly two years old so there are probably more now. We surveyed prosecutors and compiled a directory of child abuse prosecutors, which was published in June 1988. I have no idea how many specialist defense attorneys there are, and would have no way to know that.

CI: What kinds of child abuse cases get tried in criminal court?

**Kinds
of
Cases**

PETERS: Every kind, from homicide at one end of the continuum to neglect at the other end. In some states neglecting a child is a crime, and in other states it is not, depending on what the legislature has decided. It also includes various types of assault, and sexual abuse.

CI: Does one type of case predominate in the criminal system?

**Sexual
Abuse**

PETERS: Yes. In terms of cases that are actually filed and litigated, sexual abuse comprises the greatest number of cases. In terms of numbers of cases that *ought* to be, in my opinion, physical abuse and neglect should comprise the greatest number. But for a variety of reasons those cases don't find their way into criminal court as often as sexual abuse.

CI: Are criminal cases frequently referred to law enforcement agencies by child protective services?

**CPS
Referral
to D.A.**

PETERS: Again, that varies not only from state to state, but among counties within states. In some communities there is an excellent working relationship between CPS, police, and prosecutors, and they freely exchange information. In others, where the relationship is characterized by suspicion and mistrust, fewer cases are reported to law enforcement.

CI: The National Incidence studies for 1986 and 1987 indicate that the majority of demonstrable cases of abuse and neglect either were not reported or were not investigated by CPS. Is there a problem of not reporting?

Reporting

PETERS: There is clearly a problem of not reporting. The classic illustration of that is the current argument among sex offender treatment professionals. It is probably best illustrated in contemporary news by Dr. Fred Berlin, the director of the Sexual Disorder Clinic at Johns Hopkins University in Baltimore. As recently as March 4, 1990, he stated publicly in the *Baltimore Sun* that he had purposely circumvented a Maryland child abuse reporting law by telling his prospective clients he would not take them as patients unless they first went to an attorney who would refer them, and that he would then be able to hide behind the attorney-client privilege and not be required to report if these patients made any admissions of having committed child abuse crimes. The Maryland Attorney General issued an opinion last month stating that Dr. Berlin's interpretation of the law was mistaken and his attempt to circumvent the law was illegal.

Fred Berlin is at one end of the continuum of sexual-abuse treaters; he has openly become an apologist for people who have committed sexual child abuse crimes in an effort to help them. There are others who are not nearly so open about their failure to report. I noticed in Andrea Sedlak's National Incidence Study that while schools learn about and report the greatest number of cases, they also fail to report the greatest number of cases. I think that has less to do with maliciousness or intentional circumvention of the law by school teachers than with the fact that teachers are not being adequately trained about their responsibilities, about the symptoms of abuse, and in the fact that they need only have reasonable suspicion to make a report, not proof beyond all doubt.

CI: Does their failure to report indicate a lack of faith in CPS response?

PETERS: In some cases I think it may. In fact, I can tell you a personal anecdote. My wife was a public school teacher for nine years. At the same time I was a professional in the child abuse prosecution system. She would occasionally come home and express frustration to me at having made a report of suspected child abuse to CPS and feeling as if the response were not what she had hoped.

Confidence in CPS

CI: Are child victims routinely referred to CPS for attention by criminal prosecutors?

PETERS: It has never been my experience that the prosecutor finds out about a case before the investigating agencies do. Usually cases that criminal prosecutors find out about are already CPS cases, so CPS knows about them before the prosecutor does. In most states, CPS is involved only in cases where a caretaker is accused or the abuse occurred within the home. The prosecutor is often involved with those kinds of cases as well. Many state laws require the police to cross-report everything, but prosecutors receive their cases from the police and from CPS. So I do not believe there is usually cross-reporting

D.A. Referral to CPS

from the prosecutor's office to CPS. However, if prosecutors are doing their job, they will have a protocol and a network established with CPS so they're regularly discussing mutual cases.

CI: What are some of the special issues related to trying crimes against children in criminal court?

Judicial Issues

PETERS: One of them is determining the definition of a "child." In the eyes of the law, a child is a person who is under eighteen years of age. There really aren't many differences between dealing with the average seventeen-year-old witness and the average twenty-five-year-old witness. If by "child" you mean a very young child—a three-, four-, five-, or six-year-old—then you are dealing with issues of competency: the child's ability to recall accurately details of what happened to him in the past, to understand simple questions about them and then answer those questions.

One of the greatest challenges in handling child abuse cases is dealing with the developmental differences between children and adults. One of the challenges in getting a fair shake for child victims is the failure of judges and others in court to understand these differences, although things are gradually changing as more training is available.

Juvenile Witnesses

For instance, infants and toddlers present a unique set of problems. Obviously, these children are either preverbal or just learning to communicate with words. Since they are unable to give a verbal account of what happened, cases must be proven with evidence other than the victim's testimony. That means we must have photographs or eyewitnesses along with medical testimony or behavioral symptoms or there will be no case. There have been a few notable successes with cases involving infants and toddlers, but they are few and far between. That makes infants and toddlers a particularly vulnerable class of victim because offenders can act with little fear of detection.

Preschool Witnesses

Preschoolers present a different set of challenges. They have developing verbal skills and can often accurately remember central information about important events in their life, including incidents of abuse. However, their developmental level makes them vulnerable in a different sense than infants and toddlers. Three- to six-year-olds do not yet think like adults. Their responses are very concrete. They have trouble providing accurate information regarding the sequence of events. They omit facts and may fill in gaps by embellishing or adding peripheral details that did not occur. They have very short attention spans. During an interview or testimony, they become restless very quickly and may spontaneously change the subject. When they become bored or tired, they end the conversation by saying, "I don't know" or, "I don't remember." All of this makes them very difficult witnesses.

Primary school children may be the best witnesses of all. Because of their increased developmental level, skilled interviewers can get a great deal more accurate information from them than from younger victims. While they are naturally curious of sexual matters, most primary school children are still "innocent" regarding the intimate details of sexuality. If they can provide details of abuse, most children this age will be believed by a jury.

Primary School Witnesses

Teenage victims, on the other hand, can present a completely different set of problems. Many teens are sexually active with peers to some degree and most are well aware of sexual matters. They lack the "innocence" of the younger child. Developmentally, most teens are able to recall and discuss events the same as an adult. Emotionally, however, they may be rebellious, hostile, embarrassed, or otherwise unwilling to cooperate with the court. Conflicts with authority are a normal part of teen life, but they also detract from the teen's credibility. Teenage boys, in particular, are the most difficult and uncooperative of child witnesses because of their reluctance to even discuss victimization. I have seen cases where we had conclusive photographic evidence of the abuse and a confession from the suspect, yet the young man still denied he was a victim. This is especially true when the youngster was the "active" partner with an older man or woman.

Teenage Witnesses

CI: In criminal court, except in cases involving such charges as statutory rape, is a child victim normally considered just as any other victim?

PETERS: I hope that is changing. Slowly courts are learning that young children should not be treated just as any witness. In the case of adolescents, as I said, the older they get, the less cognitive difference there is between them and adult witnesses. Let me illustrate that. I received a phone call today from a district attorney in Enterprise, Oregon. This is a rural D.A.; he may have one assistant in his office. He has a case coming up involving a six-year-old who went through brutal sadomasochistic abuse that included some very bizarre and frightening behavior, not only sexual abuse but also hanging her by her wrists. This child is terrified to testify in the presence of the

Court Attitude Toward Juveniles

defendant. This district attorney is concerned with whether or not he can use closed-circuit television or have the child testify behind a screen or one-way mirror. I suggested to him that, from the point of view of future appeals, it would be safer persuading the court to rearrange the courtroom so that the child is in a position where she doesn't have to look eyeball-to-eyeball at the defendant than to use a screen or closed circuit television. I suggested that she could sit in a chair directly in front of the jury box, with the attorney who is questioning her sitting nearby and the defendant in a corner somewhere where she is not in a position to see him. Of course she needs to know he is there, but she does not have to look at him. I think that judges are becoming more sensitive to the fact that very young children should not be treated just as adult witnesses are. There's a very good book written by Judge Charles Schudson and Billie Wright Dziech called *On Trial: America's Courts and Their Treatment of Sexually Abused Children* (1989) that discusses a lot of the alternatives judges can use in their courtrooms to make them more friendly to children.

CI: One aspect of that issue is the right of the accused to confront the accuser, who would often be the child. What does "confront" mean in this context? Perhaps that's a case for the Supreme Court.

Sixth Amendment

PETERS: There is a case that is going to be argued before the Supreme Court this month [April 1990] called *Craig* v. *Maryland*. That case involved one-way, closed-circuit testimony where the suspect could see the children but the children could not see the suspect. The case may decide that issue, but it is not going to resolve whether other techniques that may be less restrictive will be permitted.

CI: Is there uniformity among state statutes on child abuse?

Uniformity of State Statutes

PETERS: No, they are not at all uniform. Let me illustrate. There is a place in the northeastern corner of Oregon where, if you take one step to the north, you will be in Washington State and, if you take one step to the East, you will be in Idaho. Ordinarily, of course, that kind of trivia is of interest only to people who are into games, or maybe mapmakers, or people who collect the taxes for those counties or states. But if you are a person who has committed a sexual crime against a child—say you've fondled the breasts of a thirteen-year-old— if you are in Idaho, you could get up to life for the crime of "lewd and lascivious contact with a minor." If you are in the state of Washington, that crime is called "indecent liberties," and you could get up to ten years with a presumptive actual sentence of one to three months in county jail. And if you are in the state of Oregon, the crime is misdemeanor sexual abuse and you can get no more than a year. I guess the question is: Does that mean the child in Idaho is going to be very severely traumatized and damaged and the child in Oregon will not? Can we decide penalties by zip codes? Conduct which could result in a death sentence in Mississippi or Florida is very likely to result in a sentence of county jail, probation, and outpatient treatment for sexual deviancy in Minnesota or Washington. So there is very little uniformity among state laws.

CI: Is there some way the laws can be made uniform?

PETERS: I don't think so. Criminal laws as well as other laws vary from state to state. There are lots of historical reasons for that. The United States Senate and the House of Representatives are currently considering a sweeping reform bill called "The Child Victim's Bill of Rights." The bill would incorporate into federal law many of the reforms that have been adopted by the states. It looks to me as if it will be the most comprehensive reform bill in the country. It will apply only to federal court, but it will be a real model. It takes the best of what states have done individually and compiles them into one piece of legislation. It will be a step forward toward making courts more accessible to children, but will have little bearing on the inequities among state penal statutes.

Uniform Code

CI: So one of the functions of it will be to provide a model for states looking to reform state laws.

PETERS: Yes. It is kind of funny to say it will be a model, because it used the state laws as its own model. But it puts the best things that the states have done into one piece of legislation.

Model Statute

CI: In your experience, do child abusers tend to receive harsher sentences than other criminal offenders?

PETERS: No. As a matter of fact, a recent study by the American Bar Association revealed that more than half of the people convicted of molesting children get probation. As a condition for that probation there usually is an order for treatment, and sometimes county jail. But more than half of them get probation. I don't see that as much different than other types of felony crimes.

Sentencing for Abusers

CI: One senses a tension between social workers and law enforcement officials that appears to be amplified in the case of child abuse, particularly when family members are involved: that is the impulse to counsel on the one hand and the impulse to punish or enforce on the other. Is that an accurate representation?

Social Workers' Views

PETERS: Partially, but not completely. Within the social work profession there is a large difference of opinion. I can illustrate that by two prominent examples. Those who subscribe to the perspective that you just mentioned, which is often referred to as the "family systems" approach to dealing with child abuse, are characterized by Dr. Alexander Zaphiris of the University of Houston. He is chairman of the social work department there, and he churns out social workers trained to believe that such things as incest, a father having sexual relations with his son or daughter, should not be treated as a crime but as a family problem and a family problem alone. His perspective is that criminal intervention is counterproductive to healing the family—that it is the whole family that is "sick," and not merely the person committing the crime.

The other side of that profession is exemplified by someone like Lucy Berliner, a clinical social worker from Harborview Medical Center in Seattle. She comes from a victim rights perspective that points the blame directly at the person who committed the acts. Her point of view is that the adult perpetrator is solely responsible for his actions. That perspective is not at all incompatible with law enforcement. Social workers who adhere to the victim rights perspective do not necessarily believe that "h-e-l-p" and "c-r-i-m-e" are mutually exclusive. I believe that prosecutors are in agreement with a large number of our colleagues in the social work profession, but there certainly are those from the helping professions with whom we disagree. I don't think it is fair to say that there is a general disagreement between prosecutors and social workers. In fact, two colleagues and I have written a law review article called "Why Prosecute Child Abuse" in which we set forth the belief of our center that prosecution and treatment are not mutually exclusive; that you need prosecution in order to have effective treatment; that most people who molest children do so because they enjoy it, and while they may have guilty feelings about it, when they are doing it they like it. They don't seek out help on their own—and therapists tell us they need a "big stick" to encourage molesters to enter and remain in treatment. That's where prosecution comes in; and the "big stick" is the threat of a long prison sentence if they don't comply with treatment requirements.

CI: So the effect of the prosecution would be to force them to treatment and not to send them to jail?

PETERS: That question assumes that punishment and treatment are exclusive of one another. In communities with treatment alternatives, the typical sentence will combine a county jail sentence, often on work release if the person is employed, with a sentence of probation which includes a condition that the person attend a comprehensive treatment program that's aimed at sexually deviant behavior. The two are not mutually exclusive. You don't just get help or get punishment; you can get both.

Treatment or Jail

CI: With convicted sexual abusers, is the rate of repeat offense different from that in other crimes?

PETERS: Recidivism rates with respect to child abusers depend on what kind of crime they commit, who the victim is, and the background of the abuser. The sex offender who has the greatest risk of recidivism is the male homosexual pedophile—that is, the male abuser who is primarily interested in children of the same sex. Dr. Gene Abel from Emory University has done studies demonstrating that people in this category have an extremely high number of victims in their history—in the hundreds. That kind of offender, the man who is interested in molesting boys, is the most dangerous, the most likely to reoffend. The treatment people say that person is the hardest to treat.

Recidivism

To illustrate the other end of the continuum, consider an eighteen-year-old high-school senior who is dating a fifteen-year-old high-school sophomore. He parks his car on lover's lane, and a policeman happens to drive up and catch them in the act. While most prosecutors with any common sense would not file the charge, in most states that eighteen-year-old high-school senior has technically "molested" a "child." Is that young man likely to be a dangerous pervert in the future? No more likely than anybody else. Should that person be prosecuted? In my opinion, unless we are talking about a date rape or something like that, I don't believe so. But *could* you prosecute him? In some states it would be a felony. So it is a dangerous oversimplification to toss around alleged recidivism rates of "child molesters" without defining what you mean.

CI: Has the increased interest in child abuse and neglect in the past fifteen years or so had an effect on criminal statutes?

Increased Awareness

PETERS: Yes. Virtually every state legislature has been asked to consider new child abuse and neglect statutes, and most have responded. Both state and federal criminal laws relating to child abuse and neglect have been modernized, as have evidence codes which pave the way for admission of more facts for the jury to consider. While much more can be done, I can say without equivocation that a child victim stands a better chance of justice today than he or she did ten years ago. Legislation that is more sensitive to the needs of child victims is only part of the reason. In addition, there is a growing awareness on the part of administrators in both police departments and district attorneys' offices that child abuse cases are important and deserve the attention of specially trained individuals. There are resources which did not exist ten years ago, such as the National Center for Prosecution of Child Abuse, to which professionals can turn for training and technical assistance on child abuse cases. This combination of better laws, more awareness on the parts of police and prosecutors, and additional resources makes today the best time in our history for a child to get a fair hearing in court.

CI: Are sufficient federal funds available to address the problem of criminal child abuse effectively?

Funding

PETERS: No. There is always a need for more federal funds. Some of the support for our center comes from federal funds. There is never enough; we are always scraping and scrimping. The federal legislation I mentioned earlier, if passed, would allocate money to provide for the training of prosecutors and judges, the creation of multidisciplinary investigation teams, and funding for CASA volunteers and guardian ad litems. It is a really good bill, and there is funding of about $35 million attached to it for fiscal 1990. That is a big step forward in terms of federal interest in dealing with this problem.

Reporting Child Maltreatment

In order to receive federal funding, states must comply with federal guidelines in maintaining a telephone line or set of lines for the reporting of child maltreatment. Listed below are numbers or other information for reporting in each state. Should one of the numbers change, the new number can be obtained by dialing directory assistance.

STATE CHILD PROTECTION AGENCIES: REPORTING PROCEDURES (*From Child Abuse and Neglect: A Shared Community Concern*, March 1989, U.S. Department of Health and Human Services).

ALABAMA
During business hours, make reports to county Department of Human Protective Services Unit. After business hours, make reports to local police.

ALASKA
Ask the operator for Zenith 4444 to make reports in-state. Out-of-state, add area code 907. This telephone number is toll free.

AMERICAN SAMOA
Make reports to the Department of Human Resources at (684) 633-4485.

ARIZONA
Make reports to Department of Economic Security local office.

ARKANSAS
Make reports in-state to (800) 482-5964.

CALIFORNIA
Make reports to county Department of Welfare and the Central

Registry of Child Abuse (916) 445-7546, maintained by the Department of Justice.

COLORADO
Make reports to county Department of Social Services.

CONNECTICUT
Make reports in-state to (800) 842-2288 or out-of-state to (203) 344-2599.

DELAWARE
Make reports in-state to (800) 292-9582.

DISTRICT OF COLUMBIA
Make reports to (202) 727-0995.

FLORIDA
Make reports in-state to (800) 342-9152 or out-of-state to (904) 487-2625.

GEORGIA
Make reports to county Department of Family and Children Services.

GUAM
Make reports to the State Child Protective Services Agency at (671) 646-8417.

HAWAII
Make reports to each island's Department of Social Services and Housing CPS reporting hotline.

IDAHO
Make reports to Department of Health and Welfare regional office.

ILLINOIS
Make reports in-state to (800) 25-ABUSE or out-of-state to (217) 785-4010.

INDIANA
Make reports to county Department of Public Welfare.

IOWA
Make reports in-state to (800) 362-2178 or out-of-state (during business hours) to (515) 281-5581.

KANSAS
Make reports to Department of Social and Rehabilitation Service area office.

KENTUCKY
Make reports to county offices in 14 state districts.

LOUISIANA
Make reports to parish Protective Service Unit.

MAINE
Make reports to regional Office of Human Services; in-state to (800) 452-1999 or out-of-state to (207) 289-2983. Both operate 24 hours a day.

MARYLAND
Make reports to county Department of Social Services or to local law enforcement agency.

MASSACHUSETTS
Make reports to area office or Protective Screening Unit or in-state to (800) 792-5200.

MICHIGAN
Make reports to county Department of Social Services.

MINNESOTA
Make reports to county Department of Human Services.

MISSISSIPPI
Make reports in-state to (800) 222-8000 or out-of-state (during business hours) to (601) 354-0341.

MISSOURI
Make reports in-state to (800) 392-3738 or out-of-state to (314) 751-3448. Both operate 24 hours a day.

MONTANA
Make reports to county Department of Family Services.

NEBRASKA
Make reports to local law enforcement agency or to local Social Services office or in-state to (800) 652-1999.

NEVADA
Make reports to Division of Welfare local office.

NEW HAMPSHIRE
Make reports to Division for Children and Youth Services district office or in-state to (800) 852-3345 (Ext. 4455).

NEW JERSEY
Make reports in-state to (800) 792-8610. District offices also provide 24-hour telephone service.

NEW MEXICO
Make reports to county Social Services office or in-state to (800) 432-6217.

NEW YORK
Make reports in-state to (800) 342-3720 or out-of-state to (518) 474-9448.

NORTH CAROLINA
Make reports in-state to (800) 662-7030.

NORTH DAKOTA
Make reports to county Social Services office.

OHIO
Make reports to county Department of Human Services.

OKLAHOMA
Make reports in-state to (800) 522-3511.

OREGON
Make reports to local Children's Services Division office and to (503) 378-4722.

PENNSYLVANIA
Make reports in-state to CHILDLINE (800) 932-0313 or out-of-state to (713) 783-8744.

PUERTO RICO
Make reports to (809) 724-1333.

RHODE ISLAND
Make reports in-state to (800) RI-CHILD or 742-4453 or out-of-state to (401) 457-4996.

SOUTH CAROLINA
Make reports to county Department of Social Services.

SOUTH DAKOTA
Make reports to local Social Services office.

TENNESSEE
Make reports to county Department of Human Services.

TEXAS
Make reports in-state to (800) 252-5400 or out-of-state to (512) 450-3360.

UTAH
Make reports to Division of Family Services district office.

VERMONT
Make reports to district office or to (802) 241-2131.

VIRGINIA
Make reports in-state to (800) 552-7096 or out-of-state to (804) 281-9081.

VIRGIN ISLANDS
Make reports to Division of Social Services (809) 774-9030.

WASHINGTON
Make reports in-state to (800) 562-5624 or local Social and
Health Services office.

WEST VIRGINIA
Make reports in-state to (800) 352-6513.

WISCONSIN
Make reports to county Social Services office.

WYOMING
Make reports to county Department of Public Assistance and
Social Services.

Checklist of Resource Material

The resources listed here are materials of general interest available from federal agencies and private organizations devoted to the issue of child maltreatment. This is not a complete list; there are many local organizations, which provide useful materials, that are not listed below, and many more materials are available from federal agencies.

The National Center on Child Abuse and Neglect is the federal agency established by the 1974 Child Abuse Prevention and Treatment Act to conduct research and collect, analyze, and disseminate information, among other responsibilities.

That agency maintains a computer database, updated annually, of journal articles, government reports and documents, monographs, books, published proceedings, descriptions of research projects, abstracts of court decisions, excerpts from statutes, and medical information related to child maltreatment. As of June 1987, the database held 14,904 records. It can be accessed via Telenet, Tymnet, Dialnet, or direct dial; the vendor is Dialog Information Services. There is a per-hour and a per-record access fee.

The Clearinghouse on Child Abuse and Neglect Information is the information resources component of the National Center on Child Abuse and Neglect. In addition to mainaining and making available databases, the Clearinghouse provides to professionals and other interested people books, films, programs, and other resource materials. Their catalogue, published seasonally, is available free by writing the Clearinghouse on Child Abuse and Neglect Information, P.O. Box 1182, Washington, D.C. 20013 or calling (703) 821-2086.

Funded by the National Center on Child Abuse and Neglect, the National Data Archive on Child Abuse and Neglect at Cornell University is, in its own words, "a centralized facility which processes and stores data sets relevant to the study of the causes, consequences, treatment, and prevention of child mal-

treatment. The purpose of the Archive is to facilitate the conduct of research and the dissemination and utilization of existing research findings. The Archive serves the needs of
researchers, practitioners, administrators, and policy makers
by making available readily accessible, high quality, computer-
ized data sets for secondary analysis and responding to specialized needs for data syntheses and analysis." While this facility
serves the needs of professionals, it maintains huge archives. For
information contact Dr. John Eckenrode or Dr. Jane Posers,
National Data Archive on Child Abuse and Neglect, Cornell
University, Family Life Development Center, E200 MVR Hall,
Ithaca, New York 14853-4401; phone (607) 255-7794.

—

Abused Children in America; Victims of Official Neglect.
A report of the Select Committee on Children, Youth, and
Families. Washington: U. S. Government Printing Office, 1987.
Available from Superintendent of Documents, U.S. Govern-
ment Printing Office, Washington, DC 20402.

—

Catalog of Child Abuse and Neglect Publications. 1989. U.S.
Department of Health and Human Services, Publication No.
25-01017.
Available free from the Clearinghouse on Child Abuse and
Neglect Information, PO Box 1182, Washington, DC 20013.
(703)821-2086.

—

*Child Abuse and Neglect and Family Violence Audiovisual Cat-
alogue.* 1989. U.S. Department of Health and Human Services,
Publication No. 21-01001.
$15.
Available from the Clearinghouse on Child Abuse and Neglect
Information, PO Box 1182, Washington, DC 20013.
(703) 821-2086.

—

Children and the Law (Washington, DC: ABA Center on Children and the Law, 1988).
$20.
Available from the ABA Center on Children and the Law, 1800
M Street NW, Washington, DC 20036
(202) 331-2250.

—

Flora Colao and Tamar Hosansky, *Your Children Should Know*
(New York: Bobbs-Merrill, 1983).

$7 including postage and handling. Make check or money order payable to Greenwich House Children's Safety Project. Available in libraries and through the Children's Safety Project, Box 30201, New York, NY 10011.

—

CWLA 1988-1989 Catalogue (Washington, DC: Child Welfare League of America, 1988).
Available free from the Child Welfare League of America, 440 First Street NW, Suite 310, Washington, DC 20001.
(202) 638-2952.

—

Highlights of Official Child Neglect and Abuse Reporting, 1986.
American Humane Association, 9720 East Hampton Avenue, Denver, CO 80231-4919.
$16 plus postage and handling.
(303) 695-0811.

—

Legal Rights of Children
(Shepherd's/McGraw-Hill: updated annually).
$90.
Available from Shepherd's/McGraw-Hill, PO Box 1235, Colorado Springs, CO 80901.
(800) 525-2474. In Colorado call collect 475-7230, Ext. 318.

—

National Center on Child Abuse and Neglect Research Symposium on Child Neglect. 1989. U.S. Department of Health and Human Services, Publication No. 20-01102.
Available free from the Clearinghouse on Child Abuse and Neglect Information, PO Box 1182, Washington, DC 20013.
(703) 821-2086.

—

Child Abuse and The Law: A Legal Primer for Social Workers
Washington, DC NCPCA, 1987. Available free from the
National Center for Prosecution of Child Abuse
103 N. Fairfax Street, Suite 200
Alexandria, VA 22314

—

President's Child Safety Partnership Final Report 1987
(Washington, DC: U.S. Government Printing Office, 1987).
Available free from National Victi ms Resource Center/NCJRS, Dept. A1F, PO Box 6000, Rockville, MO 20850
(301) 251-5525 or (800) 627-6872.

Sexual Abuse of Children: Selected Readings, 1980. U.S. Department of Health and Human Services.
$20 black and white; $35 color.
Available from the Joseph J. Peters Institute, 260 S. Broad Street, Suite 220, Philadelphia, PA 19102.
(215) 893-0600.

—

State Statutes Related to Child Abuse and Neglect: 1988.
1989. U.S. Department of Health and Human Services, Publication No. 06-88098.
$80.
Available from the Clearinghouse on Child Abuse and Neglect Information, PO Box 1182, Washington, DC 20013.
(703) 821-2086.

—

Study of the National Incidence and Prevalence of Child Abuse and Neglect: Public Use Tape with Documentation. 1987. U.S. Department of Health and Human Services, Publication No. 20-01097.
$75.
Available from the Clearinghouse on Child Abuse and Neglect Information, PO Box 1182, Washington, DC 20013.
(703) 821-2086.

—

Study of the National Incidence and Prevalence of Child Abuse and Neglect: Study Findings (Executive Summary and Final Report, 1988). U.S. Department of Health and Human Services, Publication No. 20-01099.
Available free from the Clearinghouse on Child Abuse and Neglect Information, PO Box 1182, Washington, DC 20013.
(703) 821-2086.

—

Washington Workbook for Child Advocates—101st Congress 1988-1989 (Washington, DC: Child Welfare League of America, 1989).
$22.50.
Available from the Child Welfare League of America, c/o CSSC, 300 Raritan Center Parkway, Edison, NJ 08818.
(201) 225-1900.

Directory of Organizations

Listed here are national organizations devoted to child safety and the support of children and parents in distress. Volunteer opportunities abound. This is not a complete list; there are countless agencies that address some aspect of child maltreatment, operating at the national, state, and local levels. Information about state and local groups can be obtained from the local department of social services.

—

AMERICAN ASSOCIATION FOR PROTECTING CHILDREN
AMERICAN HUMANE ASSOCIATION
9725 East Hampden Avenue, Denver, CO 80231 (303) 695-0811
Provides nationwide programs of evaluation, training, and research for improving child services. Works with other child welfare groups nationally. Sets and promotes national standards for child protection; acts as advocate for national and state legislation and policy for child protection. Maintains a data base of official reports of child neglect and abuse. Local chapters nationwide. Books and pamphlets, reports, and quarterly magazine available.

—

CHILD WELFARE LEAGUE OF AMERICA, INC.
440 First Street, NW, Suite 310, Washington, DC 20001-2085
(202) 638-2952 Promotes child welfare nationwide through its 550 public and voluntary child welfare agencies for abused and neglected children at home and in shelter care, foster programs, and residential programs. Proposes public policy initiatives, conducts research, and sets standards for child welfare programs. Runs the Children's Campaign, a national voice for a wide range of children's issues. Uses volunteer help. Books, pamphlets, and quarterly magazine available.

—

CHILDREN'S DEFENSE FUND
122 C Street NW, 4th Floor, Washington, DC 20001 (202) 628-8787 Provides advocacy for children. Engages in research,

public education, and monitoring agencies affecting child welfare and juvenile justice. Directs children's public policy network. Books, handbooks, and newsletter available.

—

CHILDREN'S SAFETY PROJECT
Greenwich House, Inc. 27 Barrow Street, New York, NY 10014 (212) 242-4140 Provides personal safety classes for ages 2 and up, including handicapped children. Provides art therapy for ages 5 and up, individual and group counseling to children who have been abused or are crime victims, as well as those coping with the murder of a family member or friend, and consultation services on detection and intervention in suspected child abuse cases.

—

CLEARINGHOUSE ON CHILD ABUSE AND NEGLECT
PO Box 1182, Washington, DC 20013 (703) 821-2086 Acts as support service of the National Center on Child Abuse and Neglect, compiling and disseminating information on child abuse and neglect. Maintains 9,500-volume library and data base accessible through DIALOG File 64.

—

NATIONAL ASSOCIATION OF COUNSEL FOR CHILDREN C. HENRY KEMPE NATIONAL CENTER FOR THE PREVENTION AND TREATMENT OF CHILD ABUSE AND NEGLECT
1295 Oneida Street, Denver, CO 80220 (303) 321-3963 Provides training and information to child advocates and works to establish a strong foundation of member practitioners from varied professions, who work with children affected by legal proceedings. Educational seminars, books, and newsletter.

—

NATIONAL CENTER FOR MISSING AND EXPLOITED CHILDREN
1835 K Street NW, Suite 700, Washington, DC 20006 (800) 843-5678, (800) 826-7653 (for the hearing impaired), (202) 634-9821 Aids parents and law enforcement agencies in preventing child exploitation and in finding missing children. Serves as a national clearinghouse of information on effective state and federal legislation for child protection. Works with individuals, parents, groups, agencies, and state and local government in locating and returning missing children.

—

NATIONAL CENTER FOR PROSECUTION OF CHILD ABUSE

American Prosecutors Research Institute, 1033 N. Fairfax Street, Suite 200, Alexandria, Virginia 22314 (703) 739-0321 Provides research, training and technical assistance to prosecutors and other professionals involved in the investigation and prosecution of child abuse cases. Has compiled a directory of prosecutors who specialize in child abuse cases and has published a definitive manual, *Investigation and Prosecution of Child Abuse.* Offers a course "Basic Training for Child Abuse Prosecutors" several times each year.

—

NATIONAL CENTER ON CHILD ABUSE AND NEGLECT

PO Box 1182, Washington, DC 20013 (703) 821-2086 Helps professionals improve services to children and families in turmoil and draws public attention to the problem of child maltreatment. Collects, analyzes, and disseminates information through the Clearinghouse on Child Abuse and Neglect. Helps states and communities develop programs and activities to identify, treat, and prevent child abuse and neglect. Operates Advisory Board on Child Abuse and Neglect, which coordinates federal efforts to combat mistreatment of children.

—

NATIONAL CHILD SAFETY COUNCIL

4065 Page Avenue, PO Box 1368, Jackson, MI 49204 (517) 764-6070 Furnishes complete child safety education programs through local law enforcement agencies and schools.

—

NATIONAL COMMITTEE FOR THE PREVENTION OF CHILD ABUSE

PO Box 2866, Chicago, IL 60690 (312) 663-3520 Works to stimulate public awareness of child maltreatment and serves as a national advocate for its prevention. Facilitates communications about program activities, public policy, and research related to child abuse. Fosters cooperation between existing and developing resources for prevention. Has local chapters. Monographs available.

—

NATIONAL COURT APPOINTED SPECIAL ADVOCATES
ASSOCIATION
909 NE 43rd Street, Suite 202, Seattle, WA 98102 (206) 328-
8588 Supports and maintains a network of programs to provide
court-appointed special advocates (CASAs) for abused and neglected children involved in juvenile dependency hearings. Provides training for new CASA programs; provides speakers;
compiles statistics.

—

NATIONAL EXCHANGE CLUB FOUNDATION FOR THE
PREVENTION OF CHILD ABUSE
3050 Central Avenue, Toledo, OH 43606 (419) 535-3232 Supports local club centers employing professionally trained volunteer parent aides who work with families in which abuse has
occurred and at-risk families. Offers parenting classes and
other support groups. Sponsors educational activities to foster
public understanding of child abuse and potential solutions.
Printed materials available.

—

NATIONAL VICTIMS RESOURCE CENTER
U.S. Department of Justice, Box 6000-AIQ Rockville, MD 20850
(800) 627-6872, (301) 251-5525, or 251-5519 Acts as a national
clearinghouse for victims' information funded by the Office for
Victims of Crime, U.S. Department of Justice. Can supply more
than 7,000 victim-related books, articles, and videotapes on
topics including child abuse and domestic violence. Maintains
national victimization statistics and conducts federally funded
studies. Will provide names, addresses, and telephone numbers
of people to contact for information and assistance.

Selected Books for Further Reading

This list provides information about a few good general books on the subject of child maltreatment. There are many books on the topic. The 1989 *Subject Guide to Books in Print* lists 278 titles under the heading of Child Abuse alone. A good university or public library will have many books that are not presently in print but that are nonetheless useful and informative.

Readers interested in intense study should consult Dorothy P. Wells, *Child Abuse: an Annotated Bibliography* (Metuchen, N.J.: Scarecrow, 1980) and Beatrice J. Kalisch, *Child Abuse and Neglect: An Annotated Bibliography* (Westport, Conn.: Greenwood, 1978). An updated annotated bibliography is badly needed.

—

Henry B. Biller, *Child Maltreatment and Paternal Deprivation: A Manifesto for Research, Prevention, and Treatment* (Lexington, Mass.: Lexington Books, 1986).

—

Rachel Calam and Christina Franchi, *Child Abuse and its Consequences* (New York: Cambridge University Press, 1987).

—

Robin Clark, *The Encyclopedia of Child Abuse* (New York: Facts on File, 1989).

—

Joel Covitz, *Emotional Child Abuse: The Family Curse* (Boston: Sigo, 1986).

—

John Crewdson, *By Silence Betrayed: Sexual Abuse of Children in America* (Boston: Little, Brown, 1988).

—

Deborah Daro, *Confronting Child Abuse: Research for Effective Program Design* (New York: Free Press, 1988).

—

Department of Health and Human Services, *Final Report*, 3 vols. (Washington, D.C.: Department of Health and Human Services, 1981).

—

Denis M. Donovan and Deborah Martin, *Healing The Hurt Child: A Developmental Approach* (New York: Norton, 1990).

—

Billie Wright Dziech and Charles B. Schudson, *On Trial: America's Courts and Their Treatment of Sexually Abused Children* (Boston: Beacon Press, 1989).

—

David Finkelhor, *A Sourcebook on Child Sexual Abuse* (Beverly Hills, Ca.: Sage Publications, 1983).

—

David Finkelhor, et al., eds., *The Dark Side of Families: Current Violence Research* (Beverly Hills, Ca.: Sage Publications, 1983).

—

Vincent J. Fontana, *Somewhere a Child Is Crying* (New York: New American Library, 1983).

—

James Haskins, *The Child Abuse Help Book* (Reading, Mass.: Addison-Wesley, 1981).

—

Jeffrey J. Haugaard, *The Sexual Abuse of Children: A Comprehensive Guide to Current Knowledge and Intervention Strategies* (San Francisco: Jossey-Bass, 1988).

—

David Hechler, *The Battle and the Backlash: The Child Sexual Abuse War* (Lexington, Mass.: Lexington Books, 1988).

—

Ray E. Helfer and C. Henry Kempe, eds. *Child Abuse and Neglect* (Cambridge, Mass.: Ballinger, 1976).

—

Ruth Inglis, *The Sins of the Fathers* (New York: St. Martin's, 1978).

—

Alfred Kadushin and Judith A. Martin, *Child Abuse: An Interactional Event* (New York: Columbia University Press, 1981).

—

Alfred Kadushin, *Child Welfare Services*, third edition (New York: Macmillan, 1980).

—

C. Henry Kempe and Ray E. Helfer, *The Battered Child*, fourth edition (Chicago: University of Chicago Press, 1987).

—

Ruth Kempe and C. Henry Kempe, *Child Abuse* (Cambridge, Mass.: Harvard University Press, 1978).

—

Jill E. Korbin, *Child Abuse and Neglect: Cross-Cultural Perspectives* (Berkeley: University of California Press, 1981).

—

Kee MacFarlane and J. Waterman, *Sexual Abuse of Young Children* (New York: Guilford Press, 1986).

—

Pamela D. Mayhall, *Child Abuse and Neglect: Sharing Responsibility* (New York: Wiley, 1983).

—

John H. Meir, ed. *Assault Against Children: Why It Happens, How to Stop It* (San Diego: College-Hill Press, 1985).

—

Barbara J. Nelson, *Making an Issue of Child Abuse: A Political Agenda Setting for Social Problems* (Chicago: University of Chicago Press, 1984).

—

Kim Oates, ed., *Child Abuse: A Community Concern* (Boston: Butterworth, 1982).

—

N. Polanski, et al., *Damaged Parents: An Anatomy of Child Neglect* (Chicago: University of Chicago Press, 1981).

—

David N. Sandberg, *The Child-Abuse Delinquency Connection* (Lexington, Mass.: Lexington Books, 1989).

—

Irving J. Sloan, *Child Abuse: Governing Law and Legislation* (New York: Oceana Publications, 1983).

—

Oliver C. S. Teng and Jamia Jasper Jacobsen, *Sourcebook for Child Abuse and Neglect: Intervention, Treatment, and Prevention Through Crisis Programs* (Springfield, Ill.: C.C. Thomas, 1988).

—

Cynthia Crosson Tower, *Child Abuse and Neglect: A Teacher's Handbook for Detection, Reporting, and Classroom Management* (Washington, D.C.: National Education Association, 1984).

—

Michael S. Wald, et al., *Protecting Abused and Neglected Children* (Stanford, Ca.: Stanford University Press, 1988).

11

Vettors

This book has been submitted to several authorities for vetting. They have made suggestions that have often been heeded, sometimes not. In every case, the vettor has been given an opportunity to provide a statement to the reader adding questions, reservations, or different perspectives to the material presented here. The vettors are in no way responsible for any errors or misrepresentations that may be included; they are largely responsible, however, for whatever merits this book may have.

Each of the interview subjects has served as a vettor, and all have offered substantial suggestions for improvement, as has David Hechler, author of *The Battle and the Backlash*.

Edwin C. Carlson, D.D.S., President of VOCAL (Victims of Child Abuse Laws) harbors basic philosophical objections to the material presented here, and, as a result, he feels that this book provides distorted information. His comments:

IN SEARCH OF A HEALTHY RESPONSE

CI: CHILD ABUSE initially sounds like a bureaucratic funding paper (Hyping questionable numbers and assuming the system is adequate) rather than being an overview of the twin problems—child neglect/abuse and the destructiveness of the current CPS response—and providing steps towards solutions.

Reporting Rate Levels or Declines: "A majority (of states) experienced leveling off or a <u>notable decline</u> in total child abuse and neglect reports in 1988." (National Comm. for the Prevent. of C/A., April 1989.)

Regardless of the numbers, large or small, child neglect and abuse is reality, from minor to severe, and needs to be adequately addressed. Child abuse hotlines also provide an invitation for false and malicious complaints, and are now overloaded with these calls. Child protection agencies are unable to provide services for children actually abused because of this misuse of the system. Thousands upon thousands of valuable lives and families are being destroyed. A false allegation of child abuse is destructive *per se*, by its very nature. The severely destructive problem of false allegations needs to be addressed.

The era of convincing the public that child abuse exists is coming to completion. What people now see is that the response is inadequate and often destructive. The failure of the system is creating its own backlash. Nationwide, CPS is in crisis.

CPS has perpetrated a fraud upon the public that CPS is competent and capable of doing what they are mandated to do. Additionally, CPS has grown out of an adversarial, prosecutorial and separationist background rather than being helping and therapeutic.

"Incestuousness" appears to exist among the "child protection cadre" with members serving on each others' boards; being the speakers at each others' "conferences"; publishing their own non-professional "journals"; and creating their own "body of literature"—frequently personal opinion/agenda or questionably "researched"—which is then quoted as reference material.

Self-serving, these agencies boost their budgets by kidnapping thousands of children from their homes before allegations are properly investigated. Children are often placed in overcrowded, dangerous environments where they are much more likely to be abused than in their homes. Families are stripped of their Constitutional right of Due Process.

CPS often does not follow legislated timelines for completing investigations. Investigators are poorly-trained, poorly supervised, and are unaccountable for their actions. Many workers have "hidden agendas" as a result of their own personal problems.

Millions of Americans have been "convicted" by CPS and "sentenced" to the "Abuse Registry" with no requirement for legal evidence, and no right to appeal or face their accusers. The family structure is being eroded, and a general clamor has arisen to correct the inequities and to improve the system.

Help for families in need of services and for neglected and abused children is an essential responsibility of a healthy society. These actions must minimally involve innocent children and families. The current amateur, entry-level, high turnover, confused, prosecutorial, adversarial, significant-number-of-pathological-workers system does more damage than it does good. It is extremely expensive and wasteful. There is now sufficient information available about what constitutes an effective and efficacious system. Efficacious meaning doing what is intended to be done.

Rather than close-up looking at the pieces of the puzzle of the current hodgepodge, emotional, knee jerk system, we need to step back and look at the whole picture, an overview of the entire field. We need generalists as well as specialists.

Common ground must be discovered by levelheaded whole-hearted people who care about children and families. A NEW MODEL can be developed that truly helps abused children (without twice and thrice abusing them in the system), and without unnecessarily involving/abusing innocent children and families.

The current system does <u>neither</u>. More than abuse/no abuse, we must ask the question "Do we have something better to offer the child?" The Michigan Supreme Court's report outlines how state intervention often makes the child's life <u>worse</u>. Separation and foster care are both damaging in and of themselves. (See accompanying "Asking the Right Questions")

THE TRADITIONAL SYSTEM ROLLS OVER CHILDREN AND FAMILIES, GRINDING THEM UP AND LEAVING THEIR MANGLED REMAINS FLOUNDERING IN ITS PATH.

The traditional system shows no concern or responsibility for the emotional and financial damage they wreak upon families and children who are falsely accused. Concurrently, the same system often fails to help truly neglected or abused children.

A continuum exists from stress-related or inadequate parenting reports to severely pathological criminals who need to be locked up forever. Rather than a continuum of responses and services, the traditional basic response is remove or leave the child. This is overreactive on one end, underreactive on the other, while being nontherapeutic and damaging on both ends and the middle.

Social services around the nation is dealing with a transition of philosophy from "rescue/remove the child" to "family preservation." In 1874 the Society for the Prevention of Cruelty to

Carlson Response Animals rescued the first child the same way as an animal, by removal from the environment. This spontaneous historical approach has persisted virtually unchallenged for 115 years.

People now know the old system does not work and is "devastatingly destructive" (Children's Rights Project). This is further documented by testimony to the U.S. House Select Committee on Children, Youth and Families, May 1988; by the recent ABC T.V. Special "The Failure of Foster Care"; and the repeated known failures of HRS. The Wall Street Journal's front page highlighted Florida's HRS as "one of the most troubled" in the nation.

Last year California rewrote its entire neglect and abuse code, with careful definitions and in-home family based services. The law details where *savings* from the new approach will be directed, into further prevention. This year the Texas Senate gave their Department of Human Services two years to restructure their system and finances, or all duties will be transferred to another agency.

Maryland's Governor Schaefer has appointed Dr. Nancy Grasmick "to study what form a new Dept. for Children and Youth Services should take." Committees on assessment, services design, information and record, legal parameters, legislation, local/state articulation, mental health/addictions, tracking, personnel, physical facilities, budget, and design have been established.

Arizona's Senator Gerald Gillespie plans to introduce a bill to shut down their current CPS for thirty days while a humane and workable system is developed. Recognizing their limitations, Vermont has reduced their system from child welfare to more purely child protection to create a "do-able" system. Alaska varies caseload size by degree of difficulty, rather than by arithmetic numbers.

Action follows funding. What legislators fund is what they get. They now fund foster care, destruction and an unworkable system. Rather than pouring more money into an aimless system, it needs to be **restructured**. The same money for the same children and families can be used for family preservation. These programs are well over 90% successful at 1/10th the cost of foster care and are virtually 100% safe for the child.

A new system will first narrow the entrance via DEFINITION and SCREENING to keep healthy families out of the system.

This has low or no cost and reduces the system's cost while increasing its effectiveness. Conservative estimates from current programs: 30% of reports can be eliminated. Scarce resources can be better applied where needed and to the problem of underreporting of valid cases. This will also spare many of the 1,320,000 innocent families per year from hurtful investigations that do not result in founded cases or even indicated.

For valid cases, we can develop a quality program for dealing with actual abuse/neglect. On a foundation philosophy of Family Preservation/Quality Alternative Living we can build a quality training program, integrated with a career ladder for case workers including credentialing, psychological screening, and proper safety/risk assessment tools integrated with a continuum of services to meet a continuum of needs. We cannot have one without the other. Categorical approaches must progress to a holistic, systems approach.

The investigative phase can be handled by specially trained police. Police have thorough training, accountability, good job retention, the public's trust and respect, and are already involved in child abuse cases. They also have a workable computer network. There is no need to duplicate this professional system with CPS' amateur entry level system (60% job turnover) and nonfunctional computer. Florida has approximately 15,000 founded cases of neglect or abuse per year (average: 224 per county). The majority are neglect of homelessness. National statistics indicate only 3% of founded cases are serious enough to require any medical attention. Law Enforcement can *triage* cases into false, criminal, or need for referral for family services.

Family Based Services in the home help families through crisis situations. These services can be provided by local organizations under local control for accountability to the community. Family Based Services are well over 90% successful, safe, time-limited, thus reducing case loads (67% closed in 90 days in Maryland). They are socially effective— 69% of California prisoners are out of foster care, 60% in Massachusets. A 97% job satisfaction rate was shown in initial federal research by the University of Iowa. Only 5% of families recycled back through the system, including delinquency, AFDC, and food stamps, in a two year study of Maryland's program.

Maryland officials testified to a U.S. Congressional Committee

Carlson Response

"that the program saves $6.2 million in foster care costs for every 1,000 children." They have been 98% successful safety keeping over 5,000 children in their own home who would traditionally have gone to foster care. The safety factor results from the diagnostic capacity of intensive involvement in the family home. Early termination of parental rights can be made in the necessary few cases. Relative placement or adoption is then given first priority and they help the parents deal emotionally with the "loss" of the child.

Family Based Services are implemented in whatever areas they are needed. If utilities are being turned off, they are paid by workers and "budget schooling" is offered. If being evicted, financial assistance is provided. If there is no food, groceries are purchased. Job training is offered when needed; parenting courses, when needed. Family counseling is offered. Substance abuse programs are available. Caseworkers carry $200 cash to solve immediate family needs. They can spend up to $6000 of "flex funds" to return families to functioning well. The total cost per average family of 3 children is $2,200. Compare this to a national average cost of $10,000 per child per year in foster care, with an average stay of three years ($90,000).

Georgia's PUP Program (Prevention of Unnecessary Placement) is shifting the use of foster care money to keep children out of foster care. They creatively drill water wells and build out-houses for mountain families rather than taking the children into foster care. Their cost: less than $1,000 per family.

Washington's Home Builders Program, established in 1974, contracts to the state for simple cases to psychiatric residential care. Across the broad spectrum, their cost is 19% of the standard state approach cost, with a 94% success, and a 100% safety record.

Adoption programs can be highly promoted for the few children removed and not placed with relatives. This will virtually eliminate the need for foster care. A national consultant says, "Due to the abuse in foster care, it can no longer be equated with safety." Shelter care and necessary foster care can then be handled by the private sector, such as the Sheriffs' Ranch, Children's Home Society, Baptist Children's Home, and others. The National Association of Foster Care Reviewers has Citizen Foster Care Review Boards in many states with detailed pilot data on four states. A Foster Care Review Board can insure quality of emergency shelter care and foster care.

The judicial system can be upgraded by certifying judges through special training in the dynamics of children and families. This is much easier than developing a Family Court System.

Short time frames can be instituted for cases involving children. "One family, one judge" can be instituted so the family stays with the same judge who knows them, throughout the case ... or throughout their children's lives. The goal of Certified Family Judges: to keep the family functioning in society. We must move from an adversarial system to a benevolent helping system such as Canada has successfully done by moving from the adversarial to the mediation approach.

A new department should be created: a Department of Family Affairs. This department will serve children, youth, family, and the elderly. There is no need to split grandparents from family. Parents are having to care for their children *and* their elderly parents as our population ages. An *elected* official should head this department. Rather than a service provider, this might be a funding agency for local programs determined by a Community Family Council.

A Community Family Council is composed of Police Chief; Chief Judge; Superintendent of Schools; media editors; church, civic and business community representatives and the new Department of Family Affairs. Their role is coordinating and integrating programs in their community on a sensitive local basis. This will redevelop a sense of community and keep all of the disciplines involved in family life working together. We can promote a one church (club or business)/one family to reinvolve these elements in keeping families healthy. This reconnects families to community and solves the isolation problem that leads to pathology.

Confidentiality of records should be replaced by confidentiality of names only. This is the process for out-of-wedlock children. With a Citizen Review Board and media access, a better balance and more effective system will be maintained.

The criminal justice system has an essential role for the truly detrimental, pathological people who should be locked up. As in Canada, we may want to look at decriminalizing minor abuse and neglect and approaching it therapeutically.

Carlson Response

Methodology and terminology will follow the shift in philosophy. Legislators must understand the whole picture. They must stop trying to patch up and bandaid the old system by pouring more money into it. Rather than get the cart before the horse by first introducing rhetoric, and terminology before methodology, they must have a change in attitude (philosophy) and structure of the system.

Like a drug addict, alcoholic or dysfunctional family, child protection leaders must admit CPS has serious problems and seek expert help. A healthy system must be created before we can help children and families in crises back to health. Proven solutions exist. We can put the pieces of the puzzle together into a dynamic new system that works for children and families. CPS should be like a hospital or antibiotic: a short, intensive, helpful interaction, then getting out of people's lives so they can get on with living in a healthier manner.

We have created cars, planes, telephones, universities, and other miracles. We can apply our creative energies to developing effective/constructive interactions with children and families. We can lead our nation in Valuing the American Family. With extreme commitment and courage, CPS can become the pride of the nation. STRONG FAMILIES MAKE A STRONG NATION.

To which part of the whole will you commit yourself?

COMMENT OF DAVID HECHLER

Hechler Response

I believe this volume is a useful introduction to a frighteningly complex subject. Its value is that it provides basic information and more, while letting you know how much larger the subject is. Then it points you to organizations and books that can help you both enhance your knowledge and use it.

I have one reservation worth mentioning here. The term "homosexual pedophile" is used more than once in the text. I believe it is grossly misleading. It feeds the false stereotype of homosexuals as predators and "recruiters." Better to refer to such individuals simply as men who molest boys or women who molest girls, since they are not necessarily homosexual--that is, attracted to adults of the same sex. Why is this important? The following article I wrote for *The San Francisco Bay Guardian* (April 18, 1990) will explain.

Child Abuse and Homophobia

By David Hechler

The question brought me up short. It came during dinner with an old college friend who had offered my wife and me a place to stay as we sojourned through Italy. He'd asked about the book on child sexual abuse I'd just finished writing, and I'd babbled for a while. Then my friend, who is gay, spat out the question—pain in his eyes, and an urgency in his voice: "Did you explain that all gay men aren't child molesters?"

I stammered agreement about the misconceptions and concluded with the journalist's fail safe parry: There wasn't enough space to include it.

Later, when I thought it over, I recalled an earlier conversation, my first with a confessed child molester. The three-hour session in a prison visiting room was laced with surprises, but one remark jumped off the page even as I copied it down.

"Sexually," said the man, who was 39, "I don't consider myself gay. I can watch gay movies and not get the least turned on."

It was months before I understood these words, and I didn't grasp their full import until I probed further, prodded by my friend's question. I believe the prisoner told the truth. He *isn't* gay. He's a pedophile—an adult sexually attracted to children.

His confusion mirrors the general public's. We assume that a man who molests boys is, by definition, gay. This false premise leads to a pair of dangerous conclusions: that gay men represent a special threat to young boys, and that men who are married or date women do not. The danger in these conclusions is that they create a false sense of anxiety *and* a false sense of security.

I can think of no better illustration than one mother's search for an after-school computer class for her son. She'd almost settled on a teacher whose classroom was attractive and who seemed competent—as did his partner. But they made her nervous, she told me, because "they just looked too swishy."

She persisted in her search, and was elated to find a man who was not only a respected teacher but was married with three children. What the mother didn't know was that he'd been sexually abusing one of his sons for years. Before he was caught, he sodomized dozens of his charges—including this woman's child.

Others may be loath to express the fear this mother voiced, but she isn't alone. "Indeed, a reputation for child molestation is one of the least enviable features of the popular stereotype of the male homosexual," observed D. J. West in his book, *Homosexuality Re-examined*.

Rarely subjected to serious scrutiny, the myth festers in wary glances and whispered gossip. Paradoxically, even as acceptance of homosexuals has increased over the years, fear that they will assault or "recruit" children has proved remarkably resilient. In a 1987 Gallup poll on attitudes toward homosexuals, 72 percent of those surveyed said homosexuals should be hired as salespersons, but only 33 percent agreed they should be hired as elementary school teachers.

While critics of homosexuals-as-teachers couch their objections in phrases like "inappropriate role models," anxiety clearly runs deeper. Yet most studies of child molesters, if better known, would assuage the public's distrust of gay men. In *Men Who Rape*, A. Nicholas Groth, a psychologist who treats sex offenders, wrote: "It has been alleged that homosexual males are especially prone to actively recruit and indoctrinate young boys into their lifestyle." Groth and coauthor H. Jean Birnbaum called that a "myth."

"Further," they continued, "it is a faulty assumption that if an adult male selects a young boy as his victim, his sexual orientation is homosexual." Nearly half their subjects were attracted exclusively to children and displayed no interest in sex with adults. "Offenders attracted to boy victims typically report that they are uninterested in or repulsed by adult homosexual relationships and find the young boy's feminine characteristics and absence of secondary sexual characteristics, such as body hair, appealing. Their focus remains on the male child as opposed to the female child, however, because they identify with the boy."

Men who molest boys frequently report they were molested themselves. If a man was abused at age eight, the theory goes, then he targets eight-year-olds to prove that he wasn't to blame, that any "normal" boy would do the same thing. Pedophiles who form relationships with adult women may do so for a variety of reasons. Some are omnivorous. Others use women to shroud their true preferences, or to access their children, or to grow their own victims.

It isn't easy to identify a pedophile. "[W]e expect a molester to be a man who displays many antisocial behaviors and in the

case of a molester whose victims are little boys, we expect him
to be a homosexual," wrote Gene Abel in a magazine article
coauthored by Nora Haflow, "But in our study," cautioned Abel,
a sex researcher and a professor of psychiatry, "we found that
most men who molest little boys are not gay. Only 21 percent of
the child molesters we studied who assault little boys were
exclusively homosexual. Nearly 80 percent. . . were heterosexual or bisexual, and most. . . were married and had children of
their own."

These are now mainstream views among those who study molesters. Their research, however, has not yet reached the public—or the media. Countless examples could be adduced, but
none more compelling than the case of Gary Little. Little was a
Seattle lawyer and part-time teacher whose rapid ascent to
Superior Court judge was trailed by persistent rumors. Insiders
knew of his "special interest" in certain boys in his classes and
his court. Television and newspaper reporters investigated, but
only snippets were aired before 1988, when the *Seattle Post-In-
telligencer* launched a six-month investigation that documented
the gossip.

On the eve of publication, Little walked into the hall outside his
chambers, put a .38 to his head and pulled the trigger. Among
the questions that followed was: Why had the media been silent
for so long?

An article in the *Columbia Journalism Review* provided answers. Little was prominent, well connected and popular. "Also
at work, several newspeople have suggested, was another fac-
tor: a failure to distinguish between pedophilia and homosexuality," explained reporter Leslie Brown. Among her sources,
Brown quoted the *Seattle Times* editor for special projects: "I
was aware that we had gotten more than one phone call that
said, Do you know that Gary Little does it with boys? It was
never clear to me that what we were talking about was Gary
Little being a pedophile, I don't think many people in 1985,
certainly not me, really fully understood what a pedophile was."
"At the same time," Brown's article concluded, "editors and
reporter alike were determined not to engage in gay-bashing."
The media, then, investigated a pedophile, equated him with a
homosexual and demonstrated sensitivity by their reticence.

As long as the public fails to distinguish homosexuals from
pedophiles, gays will be maligned and children will be at risk.
Certainly gay men have abused children (media coverage of

**Hechler
Response**
such instances isn't gay-bashing. It's crime reporting). So have Catholic priests. What's the difference? There isn't any, but the stereotype imputes to one *causation*. A man doesn't molest boys *because* he's a homosexual any more than a priest molests boys *because* he's Catholic.

Until we recognize this truth, we'll never fully understand another: The crime is about abuse, not gender.

Index